THE CAMBRIDGE
PLATONISTS

R. CUDWORTH D.D.

D Loggan del 1684.   G. Vertue Sculp

THE
CAMBRIDGE PLATONISTS

A STUDY

BY

FREDERICK J. POWICKE

ARCHON BOOKS
1971

In the work of these men, now so unjustly neglected, Dean Inge finds the greatest contribution of the English mind to the Christian philosophy of the Spirit. The restoration within the Church of the noble strain of thought for which they stand might do much, he thinks, for our current Christianity; so deficient in other-worldliness, so uninterested in sanctity, so apt to confuse social betterment with spiritual life.

EVELYN UNDERHILL in review of Dean Inge's *The Platonic Tradition in English Religious Thought.*

ORIGINALLY PUBLISHED 1926
REPRINTED 1971 BY PERMISSION OF J. M. DENT & SONS, LTD.

LIBRARY OF CONGRESS CATALOG CARD NUMBER: 79-151196
INTERNATIONAL STANDARD BOOK NUMBER: 0-208-01088-2
THE SHOE STRING PRESS, INC., HAMDEN, CONNECTICUT 06514

PRINTED IN THE UNITED STATES OF AMERICA

PREFACE

MANY years ago an old and learned friend drew my attention to the Cambridge Platonists. He seemed quite unaware of the fact that, in some of their best characteristics, they foreshadowed himself. All he did was to commend them as a rich and too much neglected field of study. He thought, in particular, that one of the men who had come under their influence—John Norris of Bemerton (1657–1711)—was a much more considerable thinker and writer than had been recognised. He gathered this, not from personal acquaintance with his books, but from Principal Tulloch's estimate of him in the second volume of his *Rational Theology in the Seventeenth Century* (1872). He advised me, therefore, if I wished—as I did—to cultivate a bit of virgin soil for myself, to concentrate on Norris. The result was that Norris became my chief intellectual interest for several years. Norris, however, was an Oxford man, a Fellow of All Souls, a High Churchman, a pronounced Tory, a somewhat bigoted controversialist—a contrast, in short, to the Cambridge men in many respects. He admired Henry More, but not exactly for what was best in him. He made much of the Platonic doctrine of ideas, but not so much in Plato's way as in that of the eccentric Malebranche (1638–1713), whose almost solitary English disciple he was proud to be. Norris the moralist, as revealed in his sermons, is a tonic; but Norris the metaphysician, as revealed in his *Theory of the Ideal and Intelligible World*, is a fantastic.

I had found time to read the Cambridge men while working on Norris, but not by any means carefully. Nor have I ever read carefully the whole of what they wrote—the whole of Cudworth's *Intellectual System of the Universe*, for example, or the whole of More's philosophical works and his dissertations on the Apocalypse. I could get no spiritual nutriment out of these, and it was spiritual nutriment that I had been told to look for. So I confined myself to Whichcote's *Sermons and Aphorisms*, John Smith's *Select Discourses*, Cudworth's great sermon before the House of Commons, and parts of his other books, More's *Divine Dialogues*, his treatise on Immortality, some of his poems, and passages of radiant beauty here and there, in the chaotic folios which he thought his masterpieces. Here the spiritual nutriment abounds, and is of noble quality. The addition of Culverwel's *Light of Nature* came as a matter of course; but Peter Sterry was a discovery, due to the description of him by Frederick Denison Maurice, and to a wellnigh accidental reading of Sterry's introduction to his *Freedom of the Will*, which led on to his sermons. Here is the passage from Maurice; and it is put here as more likely than anywhere else to catch the reader's eye. "There was a man in his (Henry More's) time who deserves to be remembered, both as a mystic and a very profound thinker; one who had many of the qualities both of Tauler and Böhme, and yet who belonged emphatically to his own age, and could scarcely have learnt his philosophy or his divinity if he had not been a contemporary of Cromwell, perhaps if he had not been his chaplain. Peter Sterry, the author of the *Race and Royalty of the Kingdom of God in the Soul*

of Man, and of a treatise *On the Will*, is one of those
men into whose writings few have looked seriously
without carrying away some impressions which they
would be very sorry to lose. Dwelling in the midst of
the Civil War, full of all the highest aspirations after a
divine kingdom which that war awakened, not surpassed by other Independents in his dislike of the
monarchy and hierarchy which he supposed had shut
out the perfect monarchy and hierarchy from the
vision of redeemed men, he was led to a different conception of the spiritual world, and of the kingdom of
darkness from that which satisfied those champions of
the Commonwealth who regarded themselves as the
saints of God, and all besides as his enemies. A struggle
of essential light with outer darkness, of original good
with evil in its first motions, sometimes overwhelmed,
sometimes elevated, his spirit. The reader may be
utterly lost in the wealth of Sterry's thoughts and
imaginations; he will seldom have to complain of poverty
or barrenness. He will always be directed to a higher
guide, who can correct the errors of the imperfect guide.
If he can make out no theory of the Will from his
suggestions and reflections, he will at least be assured that there is a good which must triumph at last.
Sterry is little read in the nineteenth century; but
a better knowledge of him would often throw light
upon the works of his contemporaries, and would
enable us to prize them more." [1]

Though this book is called a study, it makes no
pretence at all to be complete, and aims at nothing more

[1] *Moral and Metaphysical Philosophy* (1862), vol. ii., pp. 350–
351 (Library Edition).

than to express those aspects of the subject which struck me most and have seemed most relevant to my own needs. For anything like a comprehensive treatment of its historical background and context, Principal Tulloch's book is still indispensable.

But two other good books may be mentioned: E. T. Campagnac's *The Cambridge Platonists* (1901) consists of selections from Benjamin Whichcote, John Smith and Nathaniel Culverwel, with a brief introduction and notes. Nothing of Cudworth's or More's is included. This, and W. M. Metcalfe's *The Natural Truth of Christianity* (1885), drawn mostly from John Smith, provide an excellent substitute for the originals, if leisure or inclination to read these is lacking. Dr. Metcalfe's volume has also a useful memoir and a discriminating appreciation of Smith.

Four of the following chapters were written as lectures and delivered first at the United College, Bradford, by request of the late Principal Simon; and, afterwards, at Woodbrooke College, Selly Oak, Birmingham, by invitation of Dr. Rendel Harris and his successor in the Directorship of Studies, Mr. H. G. Wood, M.A.

Lastly, I beg to thank the Editor of the *London Quarterly Review* for permission to reprint the chapter on Peter Sterry, and the Editor of the *Bibliotheca Sacra* for leave to reprint (the substance of) Chapter I., and the Editor of the *Friends' Quarterly Examiner* for a like favour as regards part of Chapter VI.

FRED. J. POWICKE.

4 LANGFORD ROAD,
HEATON MOOR, STOCKPORT.
August 1926.

CONTENTS

LIST OF ILLUSTRATIONS

PROLOGUE

THE movement we are about to study was not only connected with Cambridge but also very intimately with the most Puritan and Calvinistic college of the University—Emmanuel. Its founder, Sir Walter Mildmay, obtained the charter for its foundation in January 1584, when Puritan sentiment had become at once very strong and very unpopular. Strong in parliament and in a section of the clergy and in the urban middle class, it was unpopular with the queen and the bulk of the clergy and the majority of their parishioners. Whitgift had lately (1583) succeeded Grindal as Archbishop of Canterbury—which meant violence succeeding conciliation. One of his first efforts was to put down Puritanism in Cambridge, as he had tried to break its strength in Oxford.[1] In 1584 an edition of Cartwright's translation of Walter Travers's *Disciplina* (1574)[2] by the University Press provoked him greatly. He wrote of it to Burghley in September, and got all discoverable copies of the book destroyed. This action rather strengthened than impaired the growth of the opinions which the book defended. The younger men took to them with avidity, and infected with them nearly all the colleges. From

[1] Where it had wider prevalence—Mullinger, *History of Cambridge University*, ii. p. 283.

[2] *Disciplina Ecclesiæ sacra Dei verbo descripta*. The full text of this is printed (appendix iii.) in Paget's *Introduction to the Fifth Book of Hooker's Ecclesiastical Polity* (1899). It carried immense weight with the Cambridge Puritans.

1584 to 1600 Whitgift had a rare fight on his hands, or rather a twofold fight—"One against the discipline of Calvin and another for the doctrine of Calvin."[1] And the queen was on his side, at least in the fight against the discipline. If, then, she granted Sir Walter a charter for his new college in January 1584, she cannot have known that it was intended to be a Puritan seminary; and if, later, a suspicion of the truth was conveyed to her, no wonder that "her glance rested somewhat sternly on him" when next he appeared at Court. "I hear, Sir Walter, you have been erecting a Puritan foundation," she said. "No, Madam," he replied not quite candidly, "far be it from me to countenance anything contrary to your established laws; but I have set an acorn which, when it becomes an oak, God alone knows what will be the fruit thereof."

In fact its Puritanism from the first seemed to be extreme.

"The first Master, Lawrence Chaderton (one of the translators of the Bible), who filled the office for thirty-six years, gave on more than one occasion ample proof of his sympathies with the Puritan party. Thomas Hooker, John Cotton, Thomas Shepard, and not a few other names which occupy a conspicuous place in the pages of Cotton Mather's *New England*—among them the founder of Harvard College—were some of the earliest who received their education within its walls. The tombs of earnest preachers, silenced for nonconformity while living and now resting in calmer silence in Moorfields, record in not a few instances the permanence of

[1] Mullinger, ii. 325. Whitgift's Calvinism was of the most vigorous type.

these traditions. At the beginning of the seventeenth century, the practical exemplification which the college gave of the principles laid down in the *Disciplina* was so marked as to evoke a formal protest. The chancel of its unconsecrated chapel looked north, the college kitchen east. The Society used its own form of religious service, discarded surplices and hoods, was careless even of the cap and gown, and had suppers on Fridays; while the devout Anglican was scandalised by the reports that reached him of the irreverent manner in which its members celebrated the most sacred of all the sacraments." [1]

Yet this citadel of Puritanism and Calvinism became, within the next fifty years, the cradle of a movement animated by the spirit of Plato and devoted to the golden mean in every sphere of thought and life. How can such a paradox be accounted for? Well, to account for it satisfactorily is not easy. But one or two considerations may bring some help.

1. The law of reaction must have been at work. The very stringency of Puritan and Calvinist rule would tend to create exceptions to it, and drive men of an independent or antipathetic temper into revolt. A case in point (as will be seen) was Henry More, who instinctively claimed the right to think for himself and turned impatiently against anything that hurt his conscience. More belonged to Christ's College; but men more or less like him cannot have been entirely absent from among the students of other colleges, including Emmanuel, and their presence may have gone far to explain what, after 1628, amazed the older

[1] Mullinger, ibid., pp. 313, 314.

men, viz. the ease with which their rule could be under-
mined. About that time an Anti-Puritan and Anti-
Calvinist agency entered the field in the person of
Laud's nominees to several headships—Edward Martin,
e.g. to the headship of Queens' College (1631), Richard
Love to that of Corpus Christi (1632), William Beale
to that of St. John's (1634). Their success was surprising
to Laud himself, while to his opponents it was confounding. A cry arose that Arminian errors, with their related
ecclesiastical laxities, had been accorded an open door.
But if so, the hands which opened the door were partly
on the inside. We read, in particular, of the influence
gained by Lancelot Andrewes (1555–1636), Fellow and
Master of Pembroke, whose Catechetical Lectures on
Saturday and Sunday afternoons filled the college
chapel to overflowing with undergraduates and young
curates from the country and distinguished dons. No
doubt his eloquence and fervour, and still more his
manifest saintliness, were the main attraction. But
something was due also to the largeness and reasonableness of his thought compared with the narrow dogmatism
of the regnant orthodoxy. Just when Emmanuel began
to yield to the wave of reaction is not clear. Anyhow, it
yielded, and the first to give way was its Puritanism.
This, indeed, had never been quite so extreme as it
appeared. It did not become strictly Presbyterian, still
less Independent. Even Chaderton, "though a noted
Puritan," refused to join in any cry against Prelacy.
John Preston, who followed him in the Mastership
(1622–1628), carried on his tradition; so did William
San(d)croft (uncle of William the Archbishop). Then,
after his death in 1637, came Richard Holdsworth. On

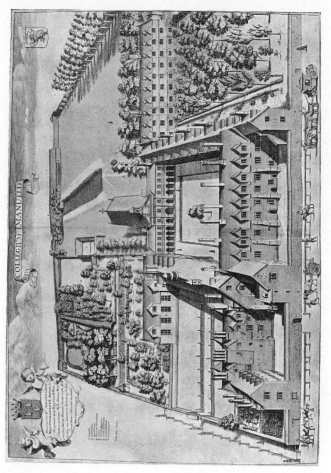

EMMANUEL COLLEGE, CAMBRIDGE
From a print by David Loggan.

him burst the storm which for years had been gathering from without. He saw it approaching when, in July 1641, he delivered his famous oration entitled "In Vesperiis Comitiorum"; and, if he voiced the mind of his college, we need no further evidence of a departure from its early Puritan attitude: "Our Church is happier far than others, who traces back her origin to no popular insurrection, has inherited no maimed and mutilated priesthood, no novel discipline soon to disappear, but whatsoever stands forth to view as confirmed by Councils and defined by ancient Fathers, and originating in Apostolic time—this she has restored, maintained, and handed down for our observance." This oration, with his pronounced Royalism and refusal to subscribe the Solemn League and Covenant, cost him his Mastership and his liberty.[1] Anthony Tuckney, who took his place, did what he could to restore that strong Puritan tone which pervaded the college at his first entrance as an undergraduate in 1613. But it is well to remember that this tone was weakening when Whichcote entered in 1626, and that he was there during all Holdsworth's time.

The Calvinism of Emmanuel was accounted its glory. When Valentine Cary, the head of Christ's College (1609–1620), taught Arminianism there is said to have been a rush of students to Emmanuel as to a refuge from the plague. Chaderton, Preston, San(d)croft, Holdsworth were never heard to strike an uncertain sound. Their purity of doctrine, and that of the college, passed into a proverb. Yet its Calvinism, also, gave way. Moreover, the signi-

[1] He was confined first in Ely House and afterwards in the Tower, but released on bail 31 October, 1645.

ficant fact is that its decay coincided with the birth of "a nobler, freer, and more generous set of opinions." Reaction and reconstruction went together. Out of the old sprang the new. And two special circumstances may have contributed to this. In the first place, Emmanuel is said to have been characterised by a more vigorous intellectual life than any other of the colleges. We are told that it long held first place in the schools. Devotion to study and learning was its fixed tradition. In this respect, says Fuller, it seemed "to overshadow the University." [1]

Surely it would be a natural result of such a quality to develop, in an unusual degree, the power and habit of robust thinking? But, in the second place, still more effectual would be the fact, if it was a fact (of which there is good evidence), that the men of Emmanuel took their creed as seriously as they took their studies, held it as a conviction rather than a creed, and tried to live by it. For then the application of their mind to it was inevitable; and some of the men, at least, would discover that *just because they were Calvinists, they must not fear becoming sceptics*. It is, indeed, historically true that the central principle of Calvinism encourages freedom of thought; if it humbles man under the mighty hand of God, it at the same time lifts him up, sets him on his feet, liberates him from all fear of human judgment, quickens and sharpens to the uttermost his sense of responsibility to God alone, emboldens him to challenge and renounce whatever draws him off from his supreme

[1] By way of illustration he mentions that, during the time of the Commonwealth, no fewer than eleven heads of other Houses came from Emmanuel. Mullinger, ii. 314.

allegiance. If, therefore, it might make him, in the sphere of politics, the most reverent of conservatives and yet the most radical of reformers, it might do likewise in the sphere of religion. It did the former when he became convinced that something already established bore upon it the signature of a divine command; it did the latter when what was believed or taught or practised seemed to him false or wrong as tested by the revealed will of God. The former, in the sphere of religion, might make him an intolerant dogmatist, while the latter might make him a ruthless iconoclast, but also a devoted seeker of the truth. And the point is that, though in the first decades of the seventeenth century the latent dogmatism of the Calvinistic principle had the upper hand, its latent progressive impulse was available for any Calvinist who came to realise its summons to his sense of individual obligation. Let any young Calvinist of Emmanuel, e.g. come to realise the presuppositions of his creed—those presuppositions in the strength of which Calvin himself shook off the authority of Rome and worked out his *Institutio*—namely, that the Will of God is supreme, that the Will of God is revealed in the Scriptures, that the Will of God can be discovered there by an honest use of reason or conscience,—let him realise these, and would he not see that they not merely furnished him with a warrant for free inquiry within the limits of Scripture, but even demanded it of him as a duty? This, it seems to me, may have been young Whichcote's experience during his undergraduate days (1626–1633). He was, as he tells us, more given to *meditation and invention* than to much reading. What he read most was the Bible; and what

B

he learnt from the Bible struck him more and more as offering a simpler and sweeter creed than that of the Calvinism in which he had been brought up; and this being so, the very fear of God inspired by his Calvinism compelled obedience to the heavenly vision. Then he found in that little society[1] which met, perhaps at his instance, in some room of the college, a number of kindred souls with whom his new conceptions could be discussed, and possibly modified under new lights. So the seed was sown of which the harvest began to show itself in contact with the succession of men who passed through his hands, while he was Tutor and Fellow of Emmanuel (1633–1643); and of which he reaped a fuller harvest in the pulpit of Trinity Church 1644–1660).

2. The last remark suggests a fact which was, at any rate, favourable to the rapid growth of a new movement. I mean the keen appetite of Cambridge for sermons and lectures—an appetite not of recent origin, but deriving itself from the days of the great Bishop of Rochester, John Fisher (1459?–1535), its chancellor and noble benefactor. It was he who built up, if he did not actually found, the great St. John's College, and endowed it with four fellowships and two scholarships, besides lectureships in Greek[1] and Hebrew. But, perhaps, his most fruitful work was done in connection with the new chair of Divinity established by the king's mother—the Lady Margaret of Richmond, of which she made him (1503) the first professor; and more especially in connection with the Lady Margaret Lectureship which, mainly

---

[1] Alluded to by Dr. Tuckney, *infra*.

[2] He is said to have set himself to learn Greek in his sixtieth year.

by his advice, the countess also set up about the same time. Its design was to supply evangelical instruction of the laity in the surrounding country and elsewhere. The preaching was to be in the vernacular, which, at that period, had almost fallen into disuse in the pulpit. And it is noteworthy that, by a clause in the constitution of the professorship, there is to be no lecturing in Lent, so that the professor and his pupils might be occupied in preaching. Before the Lady Margaret's time, Cambridge, in common with Oxford and the country generally, had little or no preaching. Fisher, as regards Cambridge, initiated a change for the better; and his action is memorable, if only as showing how the evangelistic spirit may burn in the heart of an inveterate Romanist. Nothing could reconcile him to Luther; nor could anything reconcile him to royal instead of papal supremacy; and he died a martyr for the "old cause." But, as Erasmus said, he had Christ's compassion for the unfed sheep, and did his best to make Cambridge a training-place for faithful shepherds. One wonders if Fisher may have caught fire from John Colet (1467?–1519), who in 1497 moved all Oxford by his lectures on St. Paul, whom he dealt with in modern fashion— abandoning the scholastic and allegorical interpretation of him for a free critical exposition of the obvious meaning of the text as a whole? He might have done, if not directly, yet through Erasmus, Colet's close friend and enthusiastic admirer, who taught Greek at Cambridge in 1506, and again from 1509 or 1510 to 1514. At any rate, Erasmus took note of Fisher as the bringer of new life to Cambridge. In a letter of 1521 he couples Cambridge with Paris, "because" (he says) "these two

Universities are adapting themselves to the tendencies of the new age, and receive the new learning, which is ready, if need be, to storm an entrance, not as an enemy, but courteously as a guest." In another letter, ten years later, he recalls with special delight, three colleges of the University "where youths were exercised not in dialectical wrestling matches . . . but in true learning and sober arguments, and from whence they went forth to preach the Word of God with earnestness and in an evangelical spirit, and to commend it to the minds of men of learning by a weighty eloquence." [1]

In Oxford the free spirit of Colet was stifled under the dead weight of Aristotle. In Cambridge Aristotle was less of an idol, and the spirit of Fisher had strength enough to survive; and one unfailing expression of its life was the eager recognition which Cambridge went on giving to the place and power of the living voice. The pulpit became an established throne for any preacher possessed of a message which he knew how to deliver. Thomas Cartwright (1535–1603) found it so for his militant Puritanism; so did Laurence Chaderton (1536?–1640) who for nearly fifty years preached Calvinism at the Church of St. Clements; so did Lancelot Andrewes in the Chapel of Pembroke College; so did many another. Probably such constant and expected preaching was not all to the good; but, at least, it kept minds on the alert and the intellectual atmosphere in motion, and ensured that a teacher's word should not be killed by sheer indifference. It was, therefore, no mean advantage for the new movement that its pioneers were great preachers, and that the sphere of their eloquence was in Cambridge.

[1] Mullinger, i. 507.

3. Another fact to its advantage was the change which had come over the method and subjects of study in the University. No doubt theology still held her queenly throne; but scholasticism, none the less arid for being Protestant, was on the wane—more so than in Oxford. Aristotle, as a final authority in metaphysics, physics and logic, was passing into his eclipse. Descartes, though not yet appreciated at his true significance, had his readers, and so his critics or admirers.[1] The new outlook on Nature initiated by the *Novum Organum* which Bacon, in 1620, presented to the University of Cambridge as his own *Alma Mater*, was kindling enthusiasm here and there, even if it was true that "Science and its votaries found as yet no permanent home at Cambridge."[2] Above all, what may be called the discovery of Plato and the Platonists, which followed on a wider knowledge of Greek and the reaction against Aristotle, brought to not a few of the younger men an exhilarating sense of mental liberty and enrichment. We have noticed the introduction of Greek by Erasmus in 1506, and the foundation of a Greek lectureship by Fisher at St. John's.

A further impetus to the study of Greek occurred in 1540 with the setting up of a Regius Professorship, so much so that, after two years, Roger Ascham, the professor, could write enthusiastically that Aristotle and Plato were being read even by the boys.

Then the statutes of 1549 gave a new status to the particular study of Plato by one which enjoined the

[1] His philosophy perhaps first became known in Cambridge through John Allsopp (1621), a fellow of Christ's College. Mullinger, iii. 606.
[2] Ibid., ii. 573; ibid., iii. 67.

lecturer on Aristotle to substitute readings in Pliny or
Plato for "his labours" on the former. Greek, in fact,
had become something of a fashion. It was so fifty
years later (1602) when Scaliger put the question—with
Cambridge in mind—*Quis hodie nescit Græce? sed quis
est doctus?* A smattering of Greek was widespread,
but only a few really knew it. By this time, however,
Andrew Downes (1549?–1628) had been professor for
seventeen years, and was succeeding in his purpose to
make Greek not so much widely as deeply and exactly
known. So it came to pass that Fuller, writing of the
competitors for his chair, when he resigned in 1625,
exclaims: "How much was there now of Athens in
Cambridge when (besides many modestly concealing
themselves) five able competitors appeared for the
place?" Whether or no Downes himself cultivated and
encouraged the study of Plato and Plotinus, is doubtful.
His personal preference seems to have been for the
Greek orators, especially Demosthenes. But, given the
key to them, in a sound knowledge of Greek, there were
sure to be some awakened and inquisitive minds who
would use the key with grateful diligence. No English
edition of Plato or Plotinus had yet appeared. But as
to Plato, all his works had been issued in Venice in
1522, and at Basle in 1534, and at Paris in 1578, and
at Frankfort in 1602; while as to Plotinus, the *Enneads*
translated into Latin by Marcilio Ficino (with *Por-
phyry's Life*) had been published at Florence in 1492,
and another edition of the same at Basle in 1580, and
a third, also at Basle, in 1615. Remembering that the
circulation of books in the universities of Europe was
the rule, we may be sure that copies of these or some

of them [1]—though few—would be accessible at one or more of the colleges; and thus the Platonic fire could be kindled, or, if kindled already, could be kept burning. One imagines that in the little society for free talk and discussion, which seems to have met in the common-room of Emmanuel, the relation of philosophy to theology and the relation of Plato or Plotinus to both was a favourite topic, and that Ficino's doctrine may have been welcomed as a text, viz.:

"Religion and Philosophy are identical. For Philosophy consists in the study of truth and wisdom, and God alone is truth and wisdom, so that philosophy is but religion, and true religion is genuine philosophy. Religion, indeed, is common to all men, but its pure form is that revealed through Christ and the teaching of Christ is sufficient to a man in all circumstances."

Here, at any rate, it is possible to discern, as in a glass darkly, an outline of what we meet with in Whichcote, and particularly in John Smith.

[1] On inquiry at Emmanuel College, Queens' College and the University Library, Cambridge, it appears that there is nothing to *prove* that they possessed any copy of these editions at the period in question. But copies in private, if not in college, libraries there must have been.

THE
CAMBRIDGE PLATONISTS

CHAPTER I

SOME CHARACTERISTICS OF THE CAMBRIDGE PLATONISTS

ENGLAND was never more intensely alive than in the
middle of the seventeenth century. Englishmen have
always been politicians; but then they were politicians
and theologians as well. Moreover, it was their theology
which shaped their politics. It was the conviction that
the king had a divine right to rule in Church and State
which engaged the Royalists for what is now seen to
have been an unjust cause. It was the conviction that
God's will must be done; that God's will meant the welfare of the people, and in a special sense the welfare of
their souls; that God's will could not be done so long as
any man, even though a king, stood in the way, claiming
to interpret, but often perverting, its dictates—it was
this conviction which kindled in the Puritans so stern a
passion of resistance. God was the supreme element.
At that time, if at any time in our history, God seemed
to men a living God. We need not say, as Carlyle would
seem to say, that he was a living God only to the
Puritans. A faith in God which craved to know what
was right to believe about him, and in what way it was
right to worship him; a faith which charged all actions

of the present life with momentous issues for the life to come—was not confined to Puritans. It was a possession diffused, more or less, through all parties and ranks. It was as real in Falkland as in Cromwell, in Laud as in Owen, in George Herbert as in Colonel Hutchinson. Here, surely, is the truest key to the multiplicity of sects and the fierceness of their conflict. Men do not become zealous for things about which they feel no great concern. When there sprang up swarms of "Anti-scripturists, Familists, Antinomians, Antitrinitarians, Arians, Anabaptists," it might be natural for Puritan and Prelatist alike to ban them as "the very dregs and spawn of old accursed heresies which had been already condemned, dead, buried, and rotten in their graves long ago." Nevertheless, the sudden uprising, the rapid growth, the fervent zeal of such sects bear sure witness to the dominant interest of the age. They tell of the universal craving for acquaintance with God and God's will as the secret of satisfaction and peace. In this view, the tumult and contention which, to men like Baxter, appeared so utterly deplorable, may be seen to deserve something more than denunciation. We are to God not what we seem, but what we mean. And there was scarcely a sect in those earnest days which did not mean or intend the truth.

Still, even as the contrast between the strife and chatter of the Agora, and the seclusion of the academic grove where Plato walked and talked, so seems to our imagination the contrast between the tumult of the outside ecclesiastical world and that little circle of choice spirits at Cambridge who "studied to propagate better thoughts, to take men off from being in parties, or from narrow notions, from superstitious conceits and a fierceness about opinions." What impresses one at once in these men is not so much the articles of their creed—whether political or theological—as their temper. It is the temper of the Christian philosopher met with unexpectedly, and so the more welcome. They are not recluses. They are men of affairs. They are men who give free and large expression to their thoughts in speech and writing. They can give and take in controversy. Their views are definite, are deeply rooted in principle, are never lightly changed or abandoned. But, withal, their temper—as represented especially by Whichcote, Smith, Cudworth, and More—is the perfection of "sweet reasonableness." Bitter personalities and animosities— the generally accredited weapons of theological combatants—were abhorrent to them.

"Universal charity is a thing final in religion."[1] The truly zealous serve religion in a religious temper; in zeal there is nothing tending to provocation or exasperation. Zeal for God and truth appears to others in fair persuasion and strength of argument."[2] These are words descriptive of religion as they both conceived and practised it.

It did actually affect their whole manhood. "In the understanding it was knowledge; in the life it was obedience; in the affections it was delight in God; in their carriage and behaviour it was modesty, calmness, gentleness, quietness, candour, ingenuity; in their dealings it was uprightness, integrity, correspondence with the rule of righteousness."[3] One who values spiritual

[1] Whichcote's *Aphorisms*, No. 679.   [2] Ibid., 425.
[3] Ibid., 956.

culture cannot but be drawn to the study of men like
these—even though, as is certainly not the case, they
could do little for the intellect. They were remarkable
for learning even in that learned age. They abound in
passages of "that glorious eloquence, so rich in varied
and majestic harmonies," of which Milton and Hooker
are the greatest masters. They contain numberless
examples of noble thought, so clearly and tersely
expressed as to make their writings a rich mine of
aphoristic wisdom. But their chief claim to live, and their
chief use, lies in the fact that the reader who puts himself under their influence soon comes to feel, as Plato
said, that the soul is a winged creature whose proper
home is not the flats and mists of earth, but the pure
and open heavens; is not the perishable things of sense
but the eternal truths, the unfading hopes and ideals
of a divinely nurtured life.

My aim in this introduction is to describe some
general characteristics of these men; and the first is
indicated by what has become their historic name—
Christian Platonists. How far is the name appropriate?
Well, Whichcote and his fellows certainly read Plato,
but they read Plotinus far more,[1] and found in him a
welcome confirmation of some of their leading ideas,
though they did not derive these from him. Thus, com-
paring what they taught with Dean Inge's summary[2]
of Neo-Platonic doctrine, we cannot miss close resem-
blances. For example, Neo-Platonism gives us a clear

[1] Plato, 427–347 B.C.; Plotinus, A.D. 205–270. Six hundred
years of growth and decay lie between the two; but of this fact
they seemed unaware or careless. Their use of either was quite
uncritical in the modern sense and did not need to be otherwise
for their mainly practical purpose.

[2] *Philosophy of Plotinus*, vol. ii., pp. 228–232.

and definite standard of values absolute and eternal. So the Cambridge men emphasised the immutable principles of morality.

Neo-Platonism respects science and every other activity of human reason. Its idealism is rational and sane throughout. The supremacy of reason is a favourite theme; and so it is of the Cambridge men.

Neo-Platonism asserts that " the world as seen by the spiritual man is a very different world from that which is seen by the carnal man. Spiritual things are spiritually discerned; and the whole world, to him who can see it, is irradiated by spirit. A sober trust in religious experience, when that experience has been earned, is an essential factor in Platonic faith. Our vision is clarified by the conquest of fleshly lusts; by steady concentration of the thoughts, will and affections on things that are good and true and lovely; by disinterestedness, which thinks of no reward; and by that progressive unification of our nature which, in the Gospel, is called the Single Eye. . . . There are three avenues to the knowledge of God and of the world and of ourselves—purposive action, reasoning thought, and loving affection—a threefold cord which is not quickly broken." So, too, taught the Cambridge men, as many a passage might be quoted to show. John Smith's " Discourse on the Knowledge of God" is keyed to this note throughout. Particularly apt in relation to their constant teaching is this—" If we see things as they are, we shall live as we ought, and if we live as we ought, we shall see things as they are. This is not a vicious circle, but the interplay of contemplation and action, of θεωρία and πράξις, in which wisdom consists. Action is the ritual of contemplation, as the dialectic is its creed. The conduct of life rests on an act of faith which begins as an experiment and ends as an experience." In one or two other respects we may trace the mark of Plotinus. Thus, the Neo-Platonic conception of sin as a pure negation appears in John Smith and is not absent from Whichcote—though they certainly did not argue like Plotinus that sin is without effect on "the inner life and soul of the sinner" and "can be driven out of the system by a course of discipline." Again, the language of the Cambridge men, sometimes, in speaking of God points to that of the Neo-Platonists "about His transcendent greatness, how He is so entirely beyond our knowledge that it is better to confess ignorance than rashly to claim that we comprehend Him." But, unlike the Platonists, they held it possible to obtain a real knowledge of God and Fellowship with Him in the way of moral obedience; and not simply in the way of an ecstasy, unattainable save to one here and there at rare moments. Further, the Neo-Platonic doctrine that the universe is an "inevitable result of the goodness of the Creator, the necessary shadow or reflection of the Infinite," seems to be echoed by the Cambridge men in what they so often say about the necessary action of God as the supreme good; but, if so, they differ from the Platonists in their emphasis on the free creative will of God. And in two vital points the Cambridge teachers are simply Christian. If it be true that there is a total absence of love in the Neo-Platonic System,[1] the contrary is true of them: for they make love the central motive of God and for man. "He

---

[1] So *Neoplatonism in Relation to Christianity* (1908), by Elsee, pp. 115, 93. But see Inge, *ut supra*, p. 232.

that dwelleth in love, dwelleth in God, and God in him,"
was a favourite text. Moreover, they acknowledged no
mediator between God and the Soul except Christ,
whereas Plotinus depicted man as standing at the foot
of a ladder which ascended to God through an infinite
series of emanations.

The dependence, then, of the Cambridge men on Neo-
Platonism was by no means slavish. It did not mould
the substance, or even the forms, of their thought, to
any great extent. They drew far more from the Bible;
and their acknowledged Master was Christ. In this
respect they repeated the experience of Augustine,
whose vivid accounts of his relations to Neo-Platonism
in the seventh book of his *Confessions* must have been
known to them. On the whole, we may say that what
interested them in Neo-Platonism was not its metaphysics, but its religious spirit and its ethical idealism.
This is clear from their manner of quoting the Platonists,
which is generally by way of illustration on some aspect
of the religious life, or some principle of moral conduct.
They do not quote them as a primary authority: this
they have already in the deliverances of conscience or
in Scripture, but only as confirmatory voices. Whichcote
seldom quotes them even in this sense; Smith and More
much more often—Smith especially; while Cudworth
is a partial exception to the others, in that some elements
of the Platonic philosophy do enter more or less into the
scheme of his thought as well as illustrative references
into his language.

A second characteristic is given in the fact that
the word oftenest on their lips was Reason. Whichcote's
free and bold use of it was the special fault charged

against him by Tuckney and others. These wished "faith to have been advanced rather than reason cried up: which is yet so frequently done that it proves nauseous." [1] Whichcote, of course, did not begin the use of the term. It had already become a sort of watchword among men inside and outside the universities who claimed to be men of light and leading. But he imparted to it a significance and sacredness which soon made it a distinguishing badge. Locke in his *Essay* opens the chapter on Reason with the remark, that "the word Reason in the English language has different significations; sometimes it is taken for true and clear principles; and sometimes for the cause and particularly the final cause. But the consideration I shall have of it here is in a signification different from all these; and that is, as it stands for a faculty in man." So with the Cambridge men, reason—though they not seldom employ it in one or other of the senses mentioned by Locke—is a faculty. As such, their conception of it was Platonic.

According to Plato, there is nothing higher in man than reason; because it answers to what is highest in God. The Divine Reason, or νοῦς, is conversant with ideas only, i.e. with the pure truth of things, the essential "forms" which shape and sustain all phenomena of sense and spirit. Human reason is capable of doing the same. Man's grandest privilege and most serious duty is to escape the mere shows of life; is to rise by means of discriminating intellectual effort and purifying moral discipline, from the confused to the clear, from that which seems to that which is. Truth is that which is; is

[1] Second letter of Dr. Anthony Tuckney to Whichcote, written in 1651.

a κόσμος—a steady, steadfast system of ideas and their relations. To know the truth in all fullness belongs to God. To know it in some measure—a measure which may be ever growing in range and distinctness—was God's gift to man, when by communicating reason He communicated to him the most genuine token of His own image. So taught Plato.

And the interpretation which the Cambridge men put on the text [1] they were so fond of quoting is of itself proof enough that they agreed with Plato. To them the "candle of the Lord" was not so much the *light* as the eye of the soul, an organ of intellectual apprehension, derived from God, and godlike. The light was the truth, evidenced to the eye of reason, as the sun's light to the eye of the body, by its very nature. Their love for that particular phrase may have arisen, certainly not from the feeling that it was their only scriptural support, but from the humility which led them to confess that the glory of knowing the truth is coupled with the fact that man's knowledge, and power to know, do not, at least on earth, amount to very much; is comparatively a feeble light, a mere beam in the darkness. All the same, its divine origin and character confer upon it a divine authority, so far as it goes. "A man has as much right to use his own understanding in judging of truth as he has a right to use his own eyes to see his way." [2] "To go against reason is to go against God; it is the self-same to do that which the reason of the case doth require, and that which God Himself doth appoint. Reason is the Divine governor of man's life; it is the very voice of God." [3] In fact, the distinction and the offence of the

[1] Proverbs xx. 27.   [2] *Aphorisms*, No. 40.   [3] Ibid., 76.

C

Cambridge men was, not that they exercised or even commended reason more than others, but only that they made it the ultimate authority.

It has often been said that a result of scholasticism was utterly to suppress and eclipse reason. In a sense, no doubt, the statement is correct—in the sense, viz. that when once doctrines were established they were forced upon the mind's acceptance without option of criticism. But it should be remembered that the process which led up to the formulating of a doctrine was a strict exercise of reason, and such an exercise as trained it to a subtilty and power that have never been surpassed. Reason was indeed the handmaid of faith— faith supplied its premises—to expound and confirm these was its assigned and only legitimate task. But in doing this it disciplined itself—" Men learned in reasoning freely to reason well." At the same time they learned, gradually, to doubt and question—to question the assumptions imposed upon them by Aristotle and the Church—to doubt whether it was really the sin it was declared to be to put these authorities to the test. Thus by the use of reason came at length the emancipation of reason. Amid the debates—theological, political, philosophical—which fill the closing years of the sixteenth and the opening years of the seventeenth century, reason developed, more and more, a habit of self-reliance. In the case of the Cambridge men it not simply claimed to be free, it boldly exhibited the credentials of freedom. It ought to be free because it is divine, "the first participation from God," is the medium, though not the source, of all the light of truth. On this broad ground—ground truly philosophical—they thought and acted consistently.

They held out a welcoming hand to the new philosophy, as it became the fashion to style the Cartesian and Baconian method. Bacon's appeal to the plain facts of sensible experience from the abstractions which, in Aristotle's name, had long stood for explanations of physical phenomena, was an entirely reasonable principle; so, too, was Descartes's principle that the universe might be accounted for mechanically, as the result of the necessary interplay of matter and the circular motion "impressed by the Supreme Agent on the particles of extended substance." How far their first awakening to the independent rights of reason may have been due to Bacon and Descartes, it is hard to say. Certainly what we are told of their precursor, Joseph Mede, that he was an enthusiastic botanist and practical anatomist, and that he turned from the "troublesome labyrinths of metaphysical inquiry to physics as a reassuring study," shows that the influence of the new philosophy was in the air. Anyhow, they were among the first to hear and heed its summons to clear the mind of idols, and look facts in the face. The one "distinct" thing which an Oxford man who wrote to a Cambridge friend for light on the new Cambridge sect could "meet with," was that they are "followers for the most part of the New Philosophy wherewith they have so poisoned that Fountain (i.e. Cambridge), that there are like to issue out very unwholesome streams throughout the whole kingdom." This is true, replies his Cambridge friend. "Aristotle and the Schoolmen are indeed out of request with them." The former's "*ipse dixit* is an argument much out of fashion."

Yet, while Whichcote and his sympathisers were sure to be on the side of a philosophy whose method was frankly reasonable, their main interest did not lie in the physical but in the theological sphere, and here it was that their reason found most congenial exercise. Into this sphere the new philosophy, as represented at least by Bacon, did not penetrate. Bacon honoured theology as the Jews honoured the Holy of holies. He thought it too sacred to enter. On this point he is a Protestant scholastic. When the Articles of Religion have been "posited," reason may then be allowed to draw inferences—"as to play a game of chess according to the rules; but the 'placets' of God are removed from question." We may sail with philosophy round the world of the sciences, but theology is not a science. Coming to it, we must "step out of the barque of human Reason, and enter into the ship of the Church, which is only able by the divine compass to direct its course. Neither will the Stars of Philosophy, which have hitherto so nobly shone upon us, any longer supply their light; so that on this theme silence is golden." "Sacred Theology ought to be derived from the oracles of God, and not from the light of nature." "Therefore, attend His will as Himself openeth it, and give unto Faith that which unto Faith belongeth." [1]

It has sometimes been said that Descartes divorced theology and philosophy in a similar way. But this is more than doubtful. He did, indeed, make his bow to the Church on all occasions—professing readiness to accept her ruling in matters of divinity. But his construction of philosophy *ab initio* took up, and was

[1] See Lib. IX., *de Augmentis Scientiarum*.

bound to take up, theology on the way. "I have always thought," he says in the dedication of his *Meditations* to the Sorbonne, "that the two questions of the existence of God and the nature of the soul were the chief of those which ought to be demonstrated rather by Philosophy than by Theology." Faith on the dictate of the Church may suffice for the faithful, but faith on the distinct evidence of natural reason is necessary for the inquirer, and was to himself, whatever he might seem to think, the only faith worth much.

The Cambridge men could not fail to differ from Bacon and agree with Descartes. Their very conception of reason as a "partial likeness of the Eternal Reason," a faculty in man akin to God's own power of apprehending truth, committed them to a philosophical treatment of theology. There could be for them no question of any necessary disharmony between reason and faith. These could not even belong to different provinces. They dwelt on the same ground—they had reference to the same objects. Faith was the mind's assent to the evidence, intuitional or inferential, which reason brought forward. Such assent, when the object was intellectual, might be hindered by prejudice, or, when it was moral, by a reluctance of the will. But the yielding it was a purely voluntary act, as much so as the admission of light by the eye or of sound by the ear. To speak of blind faith, therefore, could only mean a faith which had nothing to say for itself. And this, so far from being meritorious, was neither more nor less than self-betrayal. We can see then how justly their position entitles the Cambridge men to the name of philosophical divines. Philosophers simply—in the sense of mere searchers after truth in general—they were not. Their chief concern was the highest truth, truth religious and moral; and *that* was not a mere *quæsitum*—it was something given, something already within reach. But they were philosophic divines above any who had gone before them, or any of their own time, inasmuch as they maintained that religious truth can never contradict other truth, can never contradict itself—can, in short, never be other than rational in its source, its nature, its relations, its results. We have here the key to their whole theory and practice.

(*a*) It accounts for their view of the "natural" and the "revealed." What the regnant theology made of this distinction is well known. By the Fall, it said, man ceased to be in any living relation to God. God withdrew Himself. Man was left to his own devices. Darkness and corruption became his natural element, unrelieved by any power of self-redemption or self-enlightenment. Whatever fragment of spiritual truth he possessed was traditional—fading gleams of the glory which was his in Paradise. His intellect might converse with words and things; might extract from them a use and meaning; might frame arts and sciences; might lead him on to wealth and power and civilisation. But he was without God, and so without hope in the world. How utterly this was supposed to be the case is apparent from the strenuous endeavours of orthodoxy to prove that, if men like Plato and Aristotle did not get the truth in their writings from Adam, then it must have come to them somehow from the Hebrew Scriptures. Theophilus Gale, e.g. a rather famous Puritan and Independent of the seventeenth century,[1] was really attracted by Plato: his

[1] 1628–1678.

Puritan soul was often thrilled with admiration and delight by the noble heathen's truth and love of truth. He would fain have owned some direct operation of God in Plato, some inspiration of the Spirit. But his theology stepped in. Plato was not a Jew; therefore, outside the sphere of God's personal action: so there was nothing for it but to show that he must have "borrowed" from that sphere by roundabout ways: which Gale tried to do in two bulky volumes [1] whereon he spent the best years of his life.

There was, then, according to the current belief, no such thing as "natural" light, i.e. truth communicated to man through the medium of his natural faculties of reason or conscience. Revelation was the only source of light, and revelation was another name for the Scriptures. The Scriptures did not contain the Word of God: they *were* the Word of God: genuine, authoritative, true in every jot and tittle. All Scripture, said the Calvinist, was written under the direct dictation of the Holy Spirit, and was to be read by the Church as a living voice from heaven. So given to men, it could not possibly contain discrepancy or contradiction: to question its genuineness was simple rebellion against God. It was the one and sole rule of faith. Reason might be employed to make clear the sense—to fit text to text and deduce doctrines; but must not presume to speak or judge in its own right. Some things in Scripture—in the Old Testament particularly—might inflict a shock on the reader's sense of the right and true. This, however, did not matter. Things in Scripture were right and true, not so far as approved by reason and conscience, but simply by being there.

[1] His *Court of the Gentiles*.

Now the Cambridge men differed from this entirely. They believed in "natural light," because they believed that God had not cast men off; that the vital links between Him and them had never been quite severed. True, the Fall had drawn down reason with it. It was now "but an old MS., with some broken periods, some letters worn out; it was a picture which had lost its gloss and beauty, the oriency of its colours, the elegancy of its lineaments, the comeliness of its proportions—it was like Leah, blear-eyed." But though the "eye of reason is weakened," it is not destroyed. It can still see the light; and God on His part has given light to every man in the measure of his receptiveness. God is the ocean of light wherein all human spirits move and live. He shines in all. He shines in all continually. So far, therefore, as they *can* see Him and His truth, they may see. Moreover, there are some truths to which reason has borne witness always and in every man. If a man has failed to exercise his reason, or has gathered around it a "dark, filthy mist" of sin, these truths have been dark to him. But in nobler men like Plato they have been marvellously clear, and have filled "the whole horizon of the soul with a mild and gentle light." These are the truths, which Whichcote led the way in calling "the truths of first inscription." They are what a due reverence for the rule "Know thyself" must bring first and most plainly to view. They are the common, i.e. universal, notions of God and virtue—that God is; that He is, like our own souls, intelligent and spiritual; that He is all-wise, all-good, all-holy; that we are bound to revere, and serve, and submit to Him; that "we are under obligations to good self-government"; that "in our con-

verse one with another we ought to maintain brotherly
love, and to act with all calmness and gentleness, to do
according to the measures and rules of right and equity."
These notions God has folded up in the souls of men.
They are the Master-light of all our seeing, "the foundation of all religion," the sure guide to God and heaven.
He who knows them, though a heathen, is truly wise;
he who knows and follows them will never miss the goal.
"If," says Henry More, "thou wilt be faithful to thine
inward guide, and deal uprightly in the Holy Covenant,
thou wilt want no monitor—thy way shall be made so
plain before thee that thou shalt not err, nor stumble,
but arrive at last to the desired scope of all thy travels
and endeavours." There might be saints, then, as well
as sages amongst the heathen—ancient and modern.
Plato was one, and many others. Their Teacher and Redeemer was not Moses, but the living Father of Spirits.
Moses may have been their original in some matters of
fact relating to the history of man and the world; but
in matters of spiritual life and truth the "inspiration of
the Almighty had given them understanding."

But such being the doctrine of the Cambridge School
as to so-called "natural light," what was its doctrine
as to Scripture? Not certainly that the latter is more
divine than the former: for God, the Father of lights,
is equally the Fountain of both. But what Scripture does
is to confirm natural truth. "The written word of God,"
says Whichcote, "is not the first or only discovery of
the duty of man. It doth gather and repeat and reinforce
and charge upon us the scattered principles of God's
creation." "Therefore, these things have a double sanction from God. They are the principles of His creation,

discoverable and knowable by natural light. They are again declared and included in the terms of the covenant of grace." Next, it clears, and makes sure, things which philosophy could do no more than anticipate. Thus, Plato argued about the soul's immortality, about judgment to come, about heaven and hell, about the nature of God, but could reach no definite certainty. On these and other mysteries Christ lifts a veil. Scripture reveals the surpassing love of God. "It gives a man assurance that God is placable and reconcilable; and also declares to us in what way, and upon what terms, we may be confident that God will pardon sin and receive a sinner to mercy, viz., upon his repentance and faith and returning to God."

Here Scripture opens up a region of truth fairer than man's best dreams; the fuller light of nature is here lost in a splendour such as "eye had not seen, nor ear heard, nor heart of man conceived." Whichcote and his followers, as we have seen, did full justice to those who in their day were called "mere naturalists." But they were far from being "mere naturalists" themselves. They would not blame these—they would admit that some of them "will be the condemning of many Christians at the day of Judgment." Still, their own glory was in the grace of God in Christ. They preached about nothing so much: they preached about nothing so eloquently. They loved to show how perfectly it accorded with the worthiest conception of God: how fully it meets the deepest and sorest needs of man. To use Whichcote's phrase, all their thoughts of God were steeped in "the perfume of the angel of the Covenant."

(b) But it should be carefully noted that they ever

insisted on the end to which even the grace of God is a means. Christ was the efficient means to the final end of restoring man to a state of moral integrity. "The Grace of God that bringeth salvation hath appeared to all men, teaching us that, denying ungodliness and worldly lusts, we should live soberly, righteously, and godly in this present world." This was one of Whichcote's favourite texts: he called it a summary of all necessary divinity. A saved state, he says, is a morally sound state. All that Christ did for us is with a view to implanting a new life within us which shall bear fruit in the good works for which we were created. "The great design and plot of the gospel," says Smith, "is to open and unfold to us the true way of recourse to God; a contrivance for uniting the souls of men to Him, and deriving a participation of God to man, to bring in everlasting righteousness." "The great mystery of the Gospel," says Cudworth, "doth not lie only in Christ without us (though we must know also what He hath done for us), but the very pith and kernel of it consists in Christ inwardly formed in our hearts. Nothing is truly ours, but what lives in our spirits. Salvation itself cannot save us so long as it is only without us; no more than health can cure us and make us sound when it is not within us, but somewhere at a distance from us."

Accordingly, for the Cambridge men, the moral element in Scripture was supreme. On no plea could that element be justly set aside or lowered. However texts might be quoted, and examples adduced, from the Old Testament especially, in support of some morally questionable doctrine, or practice, they were of no account. Clear principles of truth and light—affirmed by the natural reason and confirmed by the law and purpose of the Gospel — were above all particular examples and texts of Scripture. "The *moral* part of religion never alters. Moral Laws are laws of *themselves* without sanction by will; and the necessity of them arises from the things themselves. All other things in religion are in order to these. The moral part of religion does sanctify the soul; and is final both to what is Instrumental and Instituted." [1] One can see how practical in its bearing this view was at a time when Joshua's extermination of the Canaanites, and Jael's treachery, and David's cruel treatment of enemies, were accepted and acted upon as divine precedents. The Cambridge men knew nothing of historic criticism. In theory they held the common faith that the rule of Faith embraced the whole of Scripture, and that every part of it was available for the construction of doctrine or the conduct of life. But in practice they acted as if they stood where *we* stand, and saw the books of the Bible along a line of true historical perspective. It has needed generations to persuade men that in Scripture the true Word of God is Christ; and that other voices there are only true so far as they blend harmoniously with His: nay, with many the process of persuasion has yet to do its work. But the Cambridge men may be said to have advanced instinctively to this position—mainly as the result of their unswerving fidelity to that "candle of the Lord," that natural light, which was, and is, indeed, the word within, and, therefore, could not fail to lead them past all lesser lights to close and rest in the teachings of the "Word made flesh."

[1] *Aphorisms*, No. 221.

(c) Two other consequences of their application of reason to religion are even more obvious. One is the antagonism it aroused in them towards one of the dogmas of Calvinism — predestination: *decretum absolutum*. Calvinism was, as already remarked, the ruling creed in Cambridge. Arminius had a few open advocates, and possibly a few secret sympathisers. But they were not popular. They were classed with Socinians as enemies of the faith; and it was a thrust which hurt Whichcote keenly when his friend Tuckney charged him with being "too well versed in Socinian and Arminian works" — particularly in the Remonstrants' *Apologie*. He hastened to deny the charge almost angrily, and to declare that, as to the *Apologie*, he had "never seen or heard of the Book before, much less read a tittle of it." His views were Arminian, in their general character, nevertheless. There is not one of the "five points" in which he does not agree with Arminius more nearly than with Calvin. No doubt this was why John Goodwin dedicated, chiefly to him, his *Redemption Redeemed*. The arch-Arminian saw, if Whichcote himself did not see, the whereabouts of his theological position and tendencies. But still Whichcote's Arminianism—and that too of his followers—was come to independently. Assenting as they did to the sacredness of reason and conscience, they could not come to anything else. The sheet-anchor of the *decretum absolutum*, e.g., was the supposed teaching of Scripture. Given that teaching, then it *must* be true, and its supposed effect in darkening the divine character must be endured. On the contrary, to the Cambridge men the absolute goodness of God was to their faith as the

"apple of their eye." Plato had said that God and the
good were identical; that Eternal Goodness, delighting
to communicate its own perfections, was the author of
creation; that the same goodness has spread its beams
upon all things great and small, and has focussed its
radiance in the soul of man. They had learnt from the
gospel that Plato was right that God is light; in whom
is no darkness at all, and that Christ in His fullness of
grace and truth, is the mirror of God. The divine goodness—that God "must needs be good as good can be";
"that all the amiable qualities that we see in good men
are but so many emanations from those that are in God,"
"that He is that unstained beauty and supreme good to
which our wills are perpetually aspiring, and wheresoever
we find true beauty, love and goodness, we may say,
here or there is God"; "that the only glory He seeks
through man is to behold him perfectly fashioned after
His own likeness"—this to them was an axiom of faith.
To force upon them a doctrine which virtually denied
it was a staggering insult to their spiritual reason. It
seemed to them not simply *absolutum*, but *horribile
decretum*. They resented and rejected and denounced
it with their whole soul and strength. It might have
been said of them, as it was said of the "most judicious
and pious Mr. Joseph Mede," that, "if at any time his
spirit was stirred in him, it was when he observed some
to contend with an immeasurable confidence and bitter
zeal for the Black doctrine of absolute Reprobation."
In their case, too, as in his, the sentiment of holy indigna-
tion was intensified by the evidently pernicious effects
of the doctrine on many of its adherents. For, as John
Smith says, its effect might be to make men's "brains

swim with a strong conceit of God's eternal love" to them; to fill them with "strong dreams" of being in favour with heaven, of their names being enrolled in the book of life, of the debt-books of heaven being closed, of Christ being theirs—while at the same time the "foul and filthy stains" of sin were still "deeply sunk in their souls."[1] This, of course, is not a necessary effect of the Calvinistic belief. The conception of an eternal will which begins, continues and completes the work of salvation in a human soul—the central conception of Calvinism—has nothing to do with Antinomianism so long as "salvation" is felt to be salvation from sin as the indispensable condition of eternal life. There is indeed a spring of mighty moral energy—to which the Cambridge men did scant justice—in realising that God is *the* Initiating Agent from first to last in the process of salvation; and that the human part is merely receptive, is an unstinted readiness to let God work. Examples of this were before their eyes even in Cambridge. But what mainly struck them was the prominence given to the negative, rather than the positive, side of Calvinism: to "reprobation" rather than to election, i.e. to just that side which was most dishonouring to God and, at the same time, demoralising to its advocates. Hence their protest in the name of reason and conscience was the more severe and strong!

(*d*) It was due to their exaltation of reason in religion that they were stigmatised not only as Arminians, but as Latitudinarians—a name designed to be still more reproachful. "I can come into no company of late but I find the chief discourse to be about a certain new

[1] " Discourse on Legal and Evangelical Righteousness."

sect, of the men called Latitude men "—so writes the Oxford man, who signs himself G. B., to a friend at Cambridge who signs himself S. P. The date is 1662; and S. P. in his reply tells him how the name (or rather nickname) first came into vogue some years before; how it was "pointed at" certain men of "learning and good manners" in the University—meaning Whichcote, etc.; and how it was designed to insinuate a charge of in- difference, or laxity, in religious and political faith; how, as a matter of fact, the only warrant for it was their opposition to that "hide-bound, strait-laced spirit that did then prevail." Certainly the Cambridge men were not lax in the sense of putting self-interest in the first place and fidelity to principle in the second. They had clear convictions of what seemed to them the truth — as to things theological, ecclesiastical, and political. Nor did they ever, so far as I know, do or say anything inconsistent with those convictions. But what they really did was to respect the convictions of others; to teach that within the husk of every error there was a kernel of truth worth searching for; to plead for "moderation and persuasion toward all opponents." "God applies to our faculties, and deals with us, by reason and argument. Let us learn of God to deal with one another in meekness, calmness, and reason, and so represent God." [1]

Their preference, e.g. on grounds rational and æsthetic, was for Episcopacy. S. P. tells his Oxford friend that most of them had been "ordained by bishops" —a fact which had been a sure bar to their preferment if any of them came before the Committee of Triers; that

[1] *Aphorisms*, No. 572.

they highly approved the "liturgy, the ceremonies, the government and doctrine of the Church." As to the last, particularly, there is not "any article or doctrine held forth by the Church which they can justly be accused to depart from, unless absolute reprobation be one, which they do not think themselves bound to believe." "Nor," he adds, "is it credible they should hold any other doctrine than the Church, since they derive it from the same fountains, viz. from the sacred writings of the apostles and evangelists, in interpreting whereof they carefully attend to the sense of the ancient Church by which they conceive the modern ought to be guided." In the mind of Laud, this preference for the Church narrowed itself into a fanaticism. The Church, with its liturgy, ceremonies, government, and doctrines, was divine throughout. Unity meant uniformity; schism meant any degree of departure from the one heavenly pattern. On the other hand, most Puritans were just as fanatical about their particular form of a church. Hence each side in its day of power was no less eager than the other to press the State into its service against the nonconformist.

Whichcote and his friends had not the least sympathy with this disposition. Questions touching the constitution of a church could not seem to them of primary importance. If not unimportant, they were secondary. The Church was a means, not an end. Its purpose was to make men better Christians, and thereby to carry on more effectually the work of Christ. For themselves, this end seemed best achieved in a church of which the government was Episcopal. But if others held the end best served in a church of another form, why refuse to

D

them the hand of fellowship and communion? Accordingly, when Parliament set up the Presbyterian model at Cambridge, it touched nothing in their beliefs so vital as to compel dissent, although they did dissent, "with the whole force of their intellects and energies, against the narrow, persecuting spirit of Puritanism," when this came to its "highest ascendency." So, too, although they conformed "with a general readiness" to the ecclesiastical "commands and injunctions" which followed on the "happy restitution of the Church" to the pattern they professed; yet they were equally earnest and energetic against "the narrow, persecuting spirit" which, after 1662, took possession of the bishops and clergy. They were most anxious the Church doors should be set wide open, "that mercy and indulgence should be shown towards those whose consciences would not permit them to comply with the will of their governors in some things disputable."

Their attitude in relation to differences of religious belief was similar. Amongst all parties alike there was a strong tendency—though it was strongest amongst the Puritans—to lay the chief stress on doctrine. Doctrine, or materials for the construction of doctrine, was apt to be the main thing sought for in a study of the Scriptures. Especially attractive were points of doctrine which verged on the mysterious, or had to do with subjects appealing to "implicit faith"; and especially keen was the zeal of the men who propounded, or propagated, such points against those who doubted or opposed them. Now the Cambridge men were not disposed to deny the truth of doctrines simply because they were mysterious. "Suppose there be a place of

Scripture," said Whichcote, "about some notion that doth transcend the reach of human reason, and which is knowable only by divine revelation; and divine revelation is comprehended in a form of words that I cannot fully comprehend; in this case I refer myself to God, and believe that that is true which God intended in those words. This I call an implicit faith." In this his followers were agreed with him. But they deprecated insistence on "obscure doctrine" as in any degree essential to life or practice. The essentials of religion, said they, are few; are clearly intelligible to all capacities; are such as any honest mind can apprehend; are, indeed, such as all true Christians unite in accepting. To think otherwise would be dishonouring to God Himself. "We cannot put a greater abuse upon God than to say He is obscure; that He expresses Himself darkly in that which concerns every man's duty towards Him, or happiness by Him; so that the man is at a great loss whether he understands God's meaning by His written word or not." [1] Let us then, said they, come together in that which is universally clear; in that which shows itself to be sufficient because it results in a state of faith and love toward God, and in goodness of life. Let the mysteries of Scripture be expressed in the words of Scripture without seeking to explicate them into terms and systems which are sure to evoke controversy. For "determinations beyond Scripture have, indeed, enlarged faith, but lessened charity, and multiplied divisions." [2] In case of plain, or probable, error, "let a fair allowance of patience be given to those who mean well; be ready to show them, since there is ground of expectation that in a little

[1] *Aphorisms*, No. 37. [2] Ibid., No. 981.

time they will come out of their error." For "nothing is desperate in the condition of good men: they will not live and die in any dangerous error." [1] Above all, let it be remembered that Christ was *Magister vitæ*, not *scholæ*, and he is "the best Christian whose heart beats with the truest pulse towards heaven; not he whose head spinneth out the finest cobwebs. He that endeavours really to mortifie his lusts, and to comply with that truth in his life which his conscience is convinced of, is neerer the Christian though he never heard of Christ, than he that believes all the vulgar articles of the Christian faith and plainly denyeth Christ in his life."

If this was the "Latitude" of the Cambridge men, there is less need to wonder at the resentment it encountered — considering the fierce dogmatism of the times—than at the nobleness and elevation of the spirit which prompted it, and also at the comparatively limited range of its growth and action in the Church after the lapse of two hundred years.

(*e*) Lastly, it was supposed to be an effect of their reverence for reason and the inner light, that they became pre-eminently "moral preachers." Evelyn in his *Memoirs*,[2] bewailing the neglect of moral exhortation in the Presbyterian pulpit during the Commonwealth period, says, "There was now nothing practical preached or that pressed reformation of life, but high and speculative points, and strains that few understood—which left people very ignorant and of no steady principles." Indeed, systematic instruction in the practice of "Christian virtue, obedience, purity, temperance, uprightness,

---

[1] Whichcote, *Discourses*, vol. ii., p. 20.
[2] November 2, 1656.

and holiness of will and deed" grated discordantly upon the ear of the ultra-Pauline and Augustinian claimant of irreversible election and faith irrespective of works; and was utterly denounced by the Antinomian of whatever shade as a savour of "mere morality," a "stinted" and legal spirit, Arminianism and "heathenry." That this tendency to slight—or at least this failure to press home—the claims of the moral law came to its Nemesis in the scandalous licence of the next generation is well known; and it should stand to the honour of the Cambridge divines that, though they never preached "mere morality," they did proclaim with a courage and persistence which have seldom been surpassed that "faith without works is dead." "The righteousness of faith is that powerful attractive which, by a strong and divine sympathy, draws down the virtues of heaven into the souls of men; which strongly and forcibly moves the souls of good men into a conjunction with that divine goodness by which it lives and grows." [1]

One splendid illustration of their teaching in this respect is presented by Cudworth's sermon on the text, "Hereby know we that we know Him, if we keep His commandments. He that saith, I know Him, and keepeth not His commandments, is a liar, and the truth is not in him." He preached it before the House of Commons on 31 March, 1647. That year, it will be remembered, witnessed the climax of Presbyterian influence in Parliament. It was the year when the Westminster Assembly of Divines brought its five years' session to an end; when Presbyterianism had been raised at least to a nominal supremacy throughout

[1] Smith, "Discourse on Legal and Evangelical Righteousness."

the land; when the four ordinances were passed, one of which enjoined the Covenant on all the officers of the army, etc.; when, in short, the lights of sound doctrine were at their brightest. And this was the year when Cudworth seized occasion to deliver a discourse of which the scope was, not to contend for this or that opinion, but only to persuade men to the life of Christ as " the pith and kernel of religion." Open it at any place, and only variations of the same pure strain are in your ears. Thus: " If any of you say that you know Christ, and have an interest in Him, and yet (as I fear too many do) still nourish ambition, pride, vainglory, within your breasts: harbour malice, revengefulness, and cruel hatred to your neighbours in your hearts; eagerly scramble after this worldly pelfe, and make the strength of your parts and endeavours serve that blind mammon, the god of this world; . . . deceive not yourselves, you have neither seen Christ nor known Him. . . . Let us really declare that we know Christ . . . by our keeping of His commandments; and, amongst the rest, that Commandment especially which our Saviour Christ Himself commandeth to His disciples in a peculiar manner: 'This is my Commandment, that ye love one another as I have loved you.' . . . Let us endeavour to promote the Gospel with a dove-like spirit. . . . Let us take heed we do not sometimes call that zeal for God and His Gospel which is nothing else but our own tempestuous and stormy passion. True zeal is a sweet, heavenly, and gentle flame which maketh us active for God, but always within the sphere of love."

Here, again, are some words on what he means by holiness and the law: " I do not mean by holiness the mere performance of outward duties of religion, coldly *acted over* as a task, nor our habitual prayings, hearings, fastings, multiplied one upon another (though these be all good, as subservient to a higher end), but I mean an inward soul and principle of divine life that *spiriteth* all these, that enliveneth and quickeneth the dead carkasse of all our outward performances whatsoever. . . . Again, I do not urge the law written upon tables of stone without us (though there is still a good use of that too), but the law of holiness written *within* upon the fleshly tables of our hearts. The first, though it work us into some outward conformity to God's commandments, and so have a good effect upon the world; yet we are all this while but like dead instruments of musick, that sound sweetly and harmoniously when they are *only* struck and played upon *from without* by the musician's hand, who hath the theory and law of music living within himself. But the second, *the living law of the Gospel*, the law of the Spirit of life within us, is as if the *soul* of musick should incorporate itself with the *instrument* and live in the strings and make them of their own accord—without any touch or impulse from without—dance up and down and warble out their harmonies."

So much, from just one of them, in answer to the reproach that they were moral preachers. The reproach was their glory. For its only warrant lay in the fact that they realised with extraordinary vividness that the supreme value and test of religious truth is its power to awaken in men the vision, and to quicken them with the energies, of a divine life. And let it be noted, in conclusion, that they linked life and truth in another way. It was part of their most emphatic teaching not only that truth must react on life, but also that life is the path to truth. Reason, to some extent owing to their influence, became more than ever a watchword after their time. It led to great changes for the better.

We can agree with Mr. Lecky that "the triumphs won by emancipated reason, whether we look to the political, the social, the industrial or the theological sphere, have been conspicuous and conspicuously beneficent." We can agree with him, further, that one of the things to be most desired is "a love of truth which seriously resolves to spare no prejudice and accord no favour, which prides itself on basing every conclusion on reason or conscience," and in "rejecting every illegitimate influence" [1]: including the influence of "early education." For "the fable of the ancients is still true. The woman even now sits at the portal of life, presenting a cup to all who enter in which diffuses through every vein a poison that will cling to them for ever. The judgment may pierce the clouds of prejudice. In the moment of her strength she may even rejoice and triumph in her liberty, yet the conceptions of child-hood will long remain latent in the mind, to reappear in every hour of weakness, when the tension of the reason is relaxed, and the power of old associations is supreme." [2]

This is true: is, at any rate, one side of the truth. But still one feels that there must be some sound justification for the suspicion of reason entertained by so many who have been neither unenlightened nor illiberal; and is it not this? That reason has been identified so often

---

[1] *Rationalism in Europe*, vol. ii., p. 98.   [2] Ibid., p. 101.

with a private judgment which fancied itself free from
prejudice, but was really ensnared by the fatal prejudice
of its own intrinsic ability to be an adequate measure
of all things? One recalls the Deists of the eighteenth
century. Reason was their idol of the cave. Reason
could comprehend, demonstrate, or destroy, everything.
Mysteries in religion were an absurdity; and mysteries
were whatever did not yield to the touch of logical
analysis. The result for religion was a dearth, and even
death, of spiritual belief and enthusiasm. The result
for the Deists themselves has been that, "If we except
these two (Hume and Gibbon) it would be difficult to
conceive a more complete eclipse than the English Deists
have undergone." "The shadow of the tomb rests upon
them all; a deep unbroken silence, the chill of death
surrounds them." [1]

The lesson is not that religion can ever dispense with
reason, *but* that reason is more than the logical understanding; that it includes conscience; that the insight
of conscience is the medium of the highest truth; and
that such insight is directly and continuously dependent
upon the culture of the highest religious life. To the
Cambridge teachers this fact was cardinal and central.
Thus Whichcote: "Nothing is *the true improvement* of
our rational faculties, but the exercise of the several
virtues of sobriety, modesty, gentleness, humility,
obedience to God, and charity to men."

Thus John Smith: "The Divine Truth is better understood as it unfolds itself in the purity of men's hearts
and lives, than in all those subtle niceties into which
cnrious wits may lay it forth, . . . and therefore our

[1] *Rationalism in Europe*, vol. i., pp. 191-192.

Saviour's main scope was to promote a holy life, as the best and most compendious way to a right belief. He hangs all true acquaintance with divinity upon the doing God's will."

Thus Cudworth: "If we did but heartily comply with the commandments and purge our hearts from all gross and sensual affections, we should not *then* look about for truth wholly without ourselves and enslave ourselves to the dictates of this and that teacher, and hang upon the lips of men; but we should find the great Eternal God inwardly teaching our souls, and continually instructing us more and more in the mysteries of His will."

As to Henry More, it were a small thing to say that *he* believed the same. Rather, this spiritual side of reason became the keynote of all his teaching. When he went to Cambridge he was at first possessed with a "mighty and almost immoderate thirst after knowledge —he immersed himself 'over head and ears in the study of philosophy.'" The result was a sort of scepticism from which he escaped when he was led to see "that the knowledge of things—especially the deepest *cause* of things—was to be acquired not by such an eagerness and intentness in the reading of authors," but rather "by the purgation of the mind from all vices whatsoever." Henceforth his motto was, *Amor Dei lux animæ*. Reason, he would say—reason, "the oracle of God, is not to be heard but in His holy temple—that is to say, in a good and holy man, thoroughly sanctified in spirit, soul, and body."

Here the mystic element of the Cambridge men comes into view, and is seen to be not opposed to reason, but

the outcome—fruit and flower—of its noblest activity.
"Spiritual things are spiritually discerned," i.e. are
discerned by the spiritualised reason for whose normal
and efficient development there is needed both logic and
life—keen logic, if you will, but also a pure and true life.
If thou beëst it, thou seëst it, said More. In the last
resort—was Plato's teaching—being and knowledge are
identical. At any rate, the remark of a Hibbert lecturer,
suggested by the system of Socinus, is true: "As a system
of avowed Rationalism, Socinianism was born pre-
maturely. . . . Rationalism could not have its perfect
work till Biblical, following in the track of all other
literary criticism, had accumulated such a store of
indisputable facts as would warrant settled inferences.
But even when the knowledge is accumulated, and
the inferences are drawn, the rationalists will still have
to go to the mystics, if they would learn the whole secret
of Christianity." [1]

[1] Beard's *Reformation of the Sixteenth Century*, p. 281 (Hibbert
Lectures, 1883).

CHAPTER II

§ 1. CHRISTIAN TOLERANCE

THE introductory chapter has treated of features common to the Cambridge men as a whole; but these were not equally distributed. The men were united at the root in loyalty to the principle of Reason, or the "candle of the Lord," as offering sure guidance to moral and religious knowledge; but their application of the principle was inevitably affected by differences of circumstance, temperament and genius. Hence it is possible to take each leader of the movement as illustrating more conspicuously than the others some one feature of the school in particular. Of course, the distinction must be, in a measure, arbitrary; and may be drawn too sharply. But there is ground for it nevertheless; and so, without prejudice to their general and fundamental agreement, I venture to single out Whichcote as conspicuous in his witness to the Christian tolerance of the movement; and Smith in his witness to its deep and rich spirituality; and Cudworth in his witness to its inexorable moral conscience; and More in his witness to its rational mysticism. Culverwel is added as an instance of arrested development; and Sterry as an example of its mysticism in full bloom. Under these heads the movement may be presented, with some approach to completeness.

Benjamin Whichcote, sixth son of Christopher Whichcote of Whichcote Hall [1] in the parish of Stoke, Shropshire, was born there on 4 May, 1609. Nothing is known of his boyhood. In his seventeenth year, however, he was ready for the University and entered Emmanuel College, Cambridge—a sign, perhaps, of Puritan leanings at home. He graduated B.A. in 1629, M.A. in 1633, B.D. in 1640. In 1633 he was elected a Fellow. Three years later, for some unstated reason, he was ordained deacon and priest in one day, 5 March, 163$\frac{6}{7}$,[2] and in the same year was appointed Sunday Afternoon Lecturer in Trinity Church — a post which, with brief interruptions, he kept for twenty years. Such lectures really did not differ from sermons. They were a sign of faith in the peculiar value of frequent preaching, and Cambridge was noted for them. Archbishop Tillotson records that during his time (1647–1651) he usually heard four sermons every Sunday, besides one on Wednesdays. Nowhere (he says) was the Gospel so freely preached and so absolutely without charge as then at Cambridge.

Whichcote's success as a preacher was immediate. He seems to have introduced a new style. Instead of reading

[1] In " Armorial Bearings of Shropshire Families" (Shropshire Archæological Society's *Transactions*, vol. vi. p. 224) we find: *Whichcote, Ermine 2 boars passant in pale gu.* From the visitation of 1623. In a list of the gentry of Shropshire at the visitation of 1663 there is no Whichcote among them. (Ibid., vol. iv., pp. 59 ff.)

[2] By Williams, Bishop of Lincoln.

a carefully-elaborated discourse, he spoke from a few notes fluently, easily, and sometimes colloquially. He spoke, at the same time, with intense urgency; and always on topics of living interest. So his preaching was strongly marked by what Phillips Brooks called the personal quality; and, therefore, by a freshness which stood out in welcome contrast from the traditional type.

In 1643 he married, his wife being Rebecca the widow of Matthew Craddock, a wealthy London merchant, and the first Governor of the Company of Massachusetts Bay;[1] and accepted the college living of North Cadbury, Somerset. But next year, as a consequence of the parliamentary reform of the University, he came back to be Provost of King's College—a distinction he neither sought, nor was at all eager to take. For one thing, he could not bring himself to sign the Covenant, and for another, he shrank from profiting by the loss of so excellent a person as the man in possession, Dr. Samuel Collins (1576–1651).[2] But his scruples in both these points were relieved. Dr. Collins was permitted to retain half the income, and subscription to the Covenant was not enforced.[3] Except that he was made a D.D. in 1649 and was Vice-Chancellor for 1650–1651, nothing of much visible importance seems to have befallen him before the Restoration. Then the even current of his days suffered a check. By royal mandate he had to give

[1] Tulloch, *Rational Theology*, vol. ii. 431 n.
[2] Provost since 1615; Regius Professor of Divinity since 1617. Mullinger, iii. 297.
[3] Whichcote's influence with some of the visitors is said to account for this favour and also for its extension to most of the Fellows of King's College.

up his provostship[1] and retire to the parsonage of Milton, Cambridgeshire. Two years later he went from Milton to St. Anne's, Blackfriars; but, when the great fire of 1666 destroyed his church, he returned to Milton. Finally, in 1668, he settled in London as Rector of St. Lawrence Jewry, where, for a period of thirteen years or so, he "bestowed his pains twice a week" "upon a very considerable and judicious auditory—though not very numerous, by reason of the weakness of his voice in his declining years." The end came in May 1683, "in the house of his ancient and learned friend, Dr. Cudworth, Master of Christ's College." He was buried in the chancel of his own church; and Dr. Tillotson, who had been associated with him at St. Lawrence Jewry as week-day lecturer, preached his funeral sermon. Funeral sermons are not always trustworthy. But there are two sentences which well express what everybody appears to have felt about Whichcote. "Though he had a most profound and well-poised judgment, yet he was of all men I ever knew the most patient to hear others differ from him, and the most easy to be convinced when good reason was offered; and, which is seldom seen, more apt to be favourable to another man's reason than his own." "Particularly, he excelled in the virtues of conversation, humanity, gentleness and humility, a prudent and peaceable and reconciling temper." These sentences strike the note which I wish to prolong.

[1] On the grounds: (*a*) That the office was in the King's gift and Whichcote had been elected by the Westminster Assembly. (*b*) That the Provost was required by the Statutes to be a Fellow of the College before appointment, which Whichcote was not. Dr. James Fleetwood (1603–1683), afterwards Bishop of Worcester (1675–1683), took his place. See *S. P. D.*, vol. 1660–1661 (July).

When Whichcote had been provost for eight years he found himself in sharp collision with an old and revered friend. This was Dr. Anthony Tuckney (1599–1670), Master of Emmanuel, and Whichcote's tutor for four years in his undergraduate days. He had been away from the University, except for rare and short visits, since 1629. For fourteen years his home had been Boston in Lincolnshire as assistant to John Cotton and, after Cotton's migration to New England in 1633, as his successor. He had been nominated one of the Westminster Assembly of Divines (July 1643), and had taken an active part in its work.[1]

In 1645 he was chosen to succeed Dr. Holdsworth, but continued to live in London with his family till his appointment as Vice-Chancellor three years later. Then he received a shock. The whole tone of the place seemed to be undergoing a change. He had noticed something of it as early as 1644. But now it was much more evident. Calvinism, it struck him, was yielding fast to "a vein of doctrine" which did not, indeed, call itself Arminian-ism but was certainly first cousin to that great heresy. Many "Young ones" were tainted by it. It was counten-anced by not a few of the Seniors. Whichcote, especially, was reputed to be its chief exponent. There was the usual result in such cases. The "whispering tongue that poisons truth" created vague and exaggerated rumours, suspicion, coldness. Whichcote perceived "an abatement of former familiarity and openness even on the part of his most inward hearty friends." He felt this, par-

---

[1] The Exposition of the Commandments in the Larger Cate-chism is ascribed to him.

BENJAMIN WHICHCOTE
From a portrait in Emmanuel College, Cambridge.

ticularly, when he met Tuckney. They "looked upon one another rather with shyness and fear than with former love and goodwill." Any attempts he made to discover the cause "met with reservedness." So it went on for five or six years. Then a common friend reported to Tuckney how Whichcote had said that it would surely be more straightforward to deal with him in private than to whisper against him in public. Thereupon Tuckney wrote at once; the more readily because, at the moment, he was "much exercised" in mind by a sermon of Whichcote's to which he had listened on the previous day, Sunday, 7 September, 1651. Whichcote rejoiced to have an opportunity of explaining himself, and sent an immediate reply. A second, third and fourth letter followed on both sides, eight in all [1]— with abundance of plain speaking; with fiery flashes here and there; but on the whole, with an unusual regard to the courtesies of debate. Tuckney has been described —quite truly—as "narrow, stiff, and dogmatical." But he was a man of Christian temper, all the same. He had "no skill," he says, "to hide distaste in the guise of a counterfeit smile"; nor could he do otherwise than "deal plainly" when he had cause to fear that "the truth of Christ, much dearer than dearest friend," had been, or might be, prejudiced. But it distresses him to think that he may have been unjust to Whichcote, and even have presumed to "anatomise" his life. "God help me more," he exclaims, "to search into my own heart, that I

[1] Printed by S. Salter, D.D., together with twelve centuries of Whichcote *Aphorisms*, and a prefatory account of his life, etc. (1753). Collections of his sermons were published from time to time. The best and most complete is the Aberdeen edition of 1751 (4 vols.), with Preface by the third Lord Shaftesbury.

may not be so much mistaken in the one as it seemeth I am in the other."

What were Whichcote's alleged errors? Taking them in the order in which Tuckney brings them forward, they were these:

1. Whichcote maintained that there are points of doctrines about which good men differ, and may safely differ, because they are left undetermined by Scripture. Tuckney considered this "unsafe and unsound."

2. Whichcote urged "parties" who differed from one another to confine themselves to the use of Scripture words and expressions in whose authority they all agreed; and to think less of confessions of faith and catechisms. Tuckney — fresh from the Assembly of Divines—found this still "more dangerous," and a clear sign of Whichcote's sympathy with the Arminians.

3. Whichcote pleaded for "liberty of prophesying." "Truth is Truth," he said, "whosoever speaks it, and I will readily agree with Papist, Socinian, or any, so far as he asserts it; because it is not his but God's." To which Tuckney objected that such advocacy of free speech is what distinguishes Arminians and Socinians, especially in the University. Thus Whichcote's affinity is again indicated.

4. Whichcote seemed to preach a merely subjective view of the Atonement; for he was understood to hold that "it doth not operate on God but on us"; and has for its end "not to reconcile God to us but us to God." "Divinity," remarks Tuckney, "which my heart riseth against."

5. In fine, there was a smack of the new and strange

about Whichcote's teaching generally; and Tuckney thought it the effect of bad company.

"Whilst you were Fellow here," he says, "you were cast into the company of very learned and ingenious men who, I fear—at least some of them—studied other authors more than the Scriptures; Plato and his scholars above others." Hence, "the power of Nature in morals, too much advanced; Reason too much given to it in the mysteries of faith; the Decrees of God questioned and quarrelled; Philosophers (Plato, etc.) and other heathens made fairer candidates for Heaven than the Scriptures seem to allow of; a kind of moral divinity minted, only with a little tincture of Christ added; inherent righteousness so preached, as to slight imputed righteousness, and so set forth as to be something perfectly attainable in this life; an estate of love exalted above a life of faith; and some 'broad expressions' of a depreciatory character about 'ordinances.'" Such were some of the "Cordolia" (or heart-sorrows), as Tuckney called them, which Whichcote occasioned him. The latter, alas! could not say much for his comfort. He could indeed declare that Tuckney was wrong in suspecting him of any conscious connection with Socinians and Arminians. As to Arminius himself, he had never read his *Apologia* —not a tittle of it; nay, had never, so far as he knew, seen the book, or heard of it, before. As to the Schoolmen also, he could assure him that he had read nothing at all of them for ten years; and had not spent twenty-four hours in their company "these fourteen years." As to Plato, indeed, and the Philosophers, he had certainly spent some time on them and did not regret it— nay, "heartily thanked God" for what he had found in

them, but not on this account had he "one jot less
loved the Scriptures"; on the contrary, he was sure
that had he given "less weight to Scripture" and more
to "Persons and Authority," he would have better
avoided than he has done those offences "wherewith
he is charged." As to the Atonement, moreover, Tuckney
had mistaken him. No doubt he had felt driven to lay
unusual stress on its vital relation to human righteousness, because in that relation he found it usually ignored.
But he did not deny its objective significance. He had
both said, and was convinced, that Christ "alone gave
the stop to God's just displeasure and procured (man's)
restoration and recovery." [1] Whichcote, in fact, seemed
to himself really orthodox, and failed to see why his
friend should be so much aggrieved. Tuckney, however,
from his own standpoint was quite right. The difference
between the two men *was* fundamental, was a difference
of principle. Tuckney indicated the difference in his
first letter when he cried, almost fiercely, "These appeals
of yours, on all occasions, to reason have grown
'nauseous.'" He felt the instinctive shudder of one
who should find himself face to face with a natural
enemy. For the question raised was this—What is the
test of spiritual truth? How shall we be sure that anything which claims to be divine has come from God? Is
the sanction within or without? Is the seat of authority
in one's own soul or somewhere outside us? Tuckney's
view was that of the Protestant tradition, viz. Divine
Truth is given explicitly in the Scriptures; and is *made
Divine by the simple fact of being there.* Of course, he
did not exclude reason entirely. But its place was

[1] See next section.

strictly subordinate. Faith, said he, takes the lead, and accepts wholesale, what Scripture lays down. She then calls upon reason to collect and compare its statements; to arrange them in due order; to deduce logical consequences; to clear up apparent contradictions; and to weave the whole into a system. Here the function of reason ends. To sit in judgment on the substance of what Scripture lays down is beyond her province.

Whichcote's position was just the reverse. Reason, he said, may and must come first, then Faith. "The reason of a man's mind must be satisfied; no man can think against it." Faith, when it is more than credulity, is an intelligent act. It follows reason—nay, is simply Reason herself, yielding assent to the evidence which her own activity has made clear. Whichcote maintained that his position was not new. It underlay the Reformation, whose watchword was, "To every Christian belongs the right of private judgment" (*Cuilibet Christiano est Judicium Discretionis*), and certainly he was right so far. The Reformation on its intellectual side was but an aspect of the Renascence. As the latter is a name for the rebirth of reason, the rekindling of its light, in the sphere, especially, of letters and philosophy, so the former is a name for the rebirth of reason, the rekindling of its light, in the sphere of religion. When Luther abandoned "Popes, Schoolmen, traditions, fathers, councils," on what ground did he justify himself? When the Church, whose institutions and teaching he assailed, demanded his submission to her as to the infallible voice of God, what had Luther to say? He replied that his reliance was on Scripture; and when the Church claimed that she was the guardian and interpreter of Scripture; that *she* only had authority to determine its content and meaning, what, again, did he say? He appealed to his right of private judgment. He must examine for himself, interpret for himself, decide for himself. He must stand by the convictions of his reason. Whether they were or were not according to truth, so long as they seemed true to him, he must stand by them. Thus said Luther at the supreme moment of his life, when retractation or death seemed the alternative. His plea *then* was, that what is contrary to reason is contrary to God. "For" (as he put it), "how should not that be against Divine Truth which is against Reason, and human truth?" But Luther, and still more his successors, grew doubtful of their own principle. Its seeming abuse led them to denounce its very use. When it dared to question what Luther asserted to be Scriptural; when it dared to question Scripture itself; when it dared to say that Reformers were on the way to substitute for the old idolatry of the Church a new idolatry of Creeds and a Book, then reason had to be humbled. It must learn that its light is merely "the dark and gross light of Nature"; that though it be man's distinguishing gift, it is of no moment where things Divine are concerned. "It is a quality of faith" (exclaimed Luther) "that it wrings the neck of Reason and strangles the beast—which else the whole world, with all creatures, could not strangle. But how? It holds to God's word: let it be right and true, no matter how foolish and impossible it sounds. So did Abraham take his reason captive and slay it, inasmuch as he believed God's word, wherein was promised him that from his unfruitful and, as it were, dead wife Sarah, God would give him seed. . . . So, too, do all other faithful men who enter with Abraham the gloom and hidden darkness of faith; they *strangle Reason* . . . and thereby offer to God the all-acceptablest sacrifice and service that can ever be brought to Him." [1] The reaction thus initiated and sanctioned grew apace. *Credo quia impossibile* became its motto. The result, generally, was to present the whole matter of Faith as a tissue of Mysteries; and to make of Revelation something intrinsically dark. In particular, Calvinism was the result—not the Calvinism of Calvin so much as that of his rigorous disciples who shaped it into the dominant creed. But let Reason come to its own again and this creed, with a great deal besides, would topple to the ground; and Tuckney, if not Whichcote, knew it well.

We may now attempt a brief summary of Whichcote's position.

1. Contrary to Calvinism and Hobbes, he entertained a noble view of human nature. God (he says) did not make "a sorry worthless piece fit for no use, when he made man." Man is a rational being; and in virtue of reason—the candle of the Lord within him—he is made in God's image.

2. Man's grand concern is religion; and "motion of religion doth begin with reason." Is there a God? What is His character? What are His laws? These are the great questions; and reason guides us to the answer. Thus, to the rightly reflective mind: "Every creature is a line leading to God, so that we cannot miss Him. For

---

[1] Beard's *Hibbert Lectures* (1883), p. 163, and the whole chapter on " Reason and Liberty."

the heavens declare the glory of God, and every grass in the field reveals Him." Again, to the reflective mind, goodness, the highest thing in man, must be the highest thing in God and must be derived from Him. Once more, if God be good, His laws for man must also be good; and hence man can be described as in a truly natural state only when he is truly obedient to the laws of God. "Virtue"—to use Whichcote's phrase—"is connatural and conservative to the nature of man: vice is unnatural and destructive." This is one of Whichcote's cardinal maxims.

3. The moral law on which man's well-being, and even being, depends is not hard to discover. Its essential principles are written within him. They are "truths of first inscription," more ancient than the oldest Scriptures. No Scripture inspired of God could pretend to repeal them; or do other than repeat, reaffirm, and reinforce them. This is what the Bible does. This is what Christ does pre-eminently. "The recovery of Christ is a restoration and fuller confirmation of all the principles of God's creation." His Gospel consists in the announcement from God of pardon for past transgression, if we repent; and of inward all-sufficient grace for our salvation—this, and nothing more, so far as its end is concerned.

4. The end of law and Gospel alike is salvation. But salvation is simply another name for complete goodness. Goodness, therefore, being reached, all is reached; the "plot and design" of both law and Gospel is achieved.

5. So we come to Whichcote's stronghold. From his early student days he had settled with himself that moral goodness is the best and highest thing in life: the

summum bonum; the pearl of great price. The light within declared it, so did experience, so did the noblest of human teachers, e.g. Socrates and Plato, so did the prophetic voices of the Old Testament, so—above all—did Christ. Hence the earnestness with which he set himself to "call men off" from dogmas and barren speculations to the practical bearings of their faith. For, "The first thing in religion is to refine a man's temper and, second, to govern his practice." Short of this it is "a poor slender thing and of little consideration."

6. We are now on his platform of religious tolerance. He cried to contending sects and persons—The end of law and Gospel is a character, is love out of a pure heart to whatever is lovely, noble, just and true. If this be first in fact, why not make it first in your esteem? If a man manifests the Christian temper and life, why reject him? God will receive him, why not you? The gate is too wide, you say; it would admit some who have no Christian creed and many whose Christian creed is defective; and even not a few who do not preach Christ. Whichcote's answer to the last point, considering his environment, is surely a brave one. Men (he said) may preach Christ "though they do not name Christ in every sentence, or period, of words. If men contend for the effects of real goodness and deny wickedness, *they* do truly and properly preach Christ . . . for this is the effect of Christ and *this* is Christ's business. God having raised up His Son, sent Him to bless us. How? By turning away every man from his sins. Wherefore, whosoever doth deal with men to leave off sin, preaches Christ and carries on Christ's work."

His platform, we see, is of the broadest, and it may

be said to enclose an inner and an outer circle. To the latter belong all right-minded men of whatsoever creed; and these should be an object at least of kindly regard. To the former belong as many as yield sincere assent to the essential minima of the Christian faith (as stated above), and these should be recognised as constituting the visible Church. He says expressly: "We do resolve that all they who do agree in the main parts of religion may look upon themselves as members of the same Church, notwithstanding any different apprehensions in other matters." He was not personally indifferent to questions of Church government and worship, though he says but little about them. For his own part, he preferred the Episcopal polity, and would have rejoiced if all Christians could have come to agree with him. But his ideal was not uniformity, whether ecclesiastical or theological. He was prepared to allow many forms of polity and faith. What he emphasised was moral and spiritual unity. Such unity did not need to be created. It really existed beneath divergent external forms and formulæ. All that was needed was to recognise and cherish it. Let us, he pleaded, confess our radical fellowship with Christ in faith, hope and love; and have the courage to be consistent. Let it be openly granted that everyone loyal to the essential minima—in the spirit of them—is a good man, as Christ counts goodness. Let it be granted that "there can be nothing desperate in the condition of a good man," though his errors of thought and life may be many—because he "will never willingly embrace an error"; and God, who has him in hand, will, sooner or later, guide him into all the truth. Let it be granted, accordingly, that such men must be

received as Christian brethren and be free to all the
privileges of Church membership, without any thought
af imposing upon them what, to the majority, may
oppear important as well as true, but what to their
conscience is offensive. Let all this be done for "peace
and charity"; and, meanwhile, as often as possible let
us come together and calmly review our points of
difference, and try to see how far they are material or
immaterial, in view of the Christian ideal. Finally, let
us be ready both to learn and to teach; ready to give
a reason for our own belief; and a patient, humble,
generous hearing to the reason which our brother has
to give for his.

There is a passage in one of Whichcote's sermons on
the "Unity of the Church maintained by sincere Christians " which very clearly expresses his point of view:
"Why should not *consent* in the main be more available
to concord and union than *difference* in less principal
matters prevail to distance and separation? All that
are right in the *main* are virtually informed by the same
spirit. Do I not hope another may see and acknowledge
that to-morrow which he sticks at to-day? We know
not what a day may bring forth. Days teach wisdom
and experience. Wherefore, they who understand not
alike to-day may agree to-morrow. Therefore, the
philosopher's rule is rational—"Hate now as one who
may love afterwards. Part to-day upon such terms as
you may come together to-morrow."

It hardly needs to be said that in urging Christians
to demand of one another nothing more than the "essential minima" Whichcote had no wish to depreciate
truth. Baxter did not mean to depreciate truth when

he declared himself willing to comprehend within the Church as many as accepted the Lord's Prayer, Apostles' Creed, and the Ten Commandments. Nor did Chillingworth mean to depreciate truth when he argued that "whosoever believes either the Creed or the whole of any one Gospel may be sure that he believes whatsoever is necessary to salvation and something over." Mathematicians do not depreciate truth by agreeing to start from certain axioms: for these are the germs out of which they expect to develop a whole universe of truth; and a list of fundamentals may be considered as a proposed set of theological axioms. Of course, the practical difficulty lies in the process of defining what is fundamental; and, as to this, so much at least may be said for Whichcote, that his position has stood the test of time, and is more persuasive to-day than it has ever been. Experience, if it teaches anything, teaches increasingly that whatsoever else comes next, goodness is the supreme end of life; that the spirit of goodness is the uniting spirit; and that the truths which make for goodness are, therefore, the essential truths. It is the consciousness of this which does actually form the bond of union and fount of charity among Christians of every name. It is this which supplies them with those social ideals for whose sake the churches are becoming eager to confederate and work together. It is this which has gradually dissolved the age-long prejudice that a man's mere opinions and beliefs must somehow involve the fate of his soul; that doctrinal heresy is the worst of crimes. It is this which has led us to realise that dogma, for dogma's sake, is vanity. It is this, too, which, more than anything else, has helped to liberate the devout mind from fear of free critical inquiry. So long as it seemed probable that salvation and a particular dogma were, or might be, linked together, the impulse to such fear was natural, was in some cases irresistible. But the fear vanishes when it is seen that saving truths are, as Whichcote said, just the truths which save; which really inspire and promote a reconciling temper and a sanctified life. For these truths no criticism can shake. They are among the eternal lights which "rise to perish never."

§ 2. THE CHRISTIAN REVELATION

Whichcote's sermons have much to say about the Gospel, or the Christian Revelation, and the particular use of Reason in Religion. So it may be well to illustrate these points by a brief statement, and a few selected passages. In this, as in every other essential matter, he may be trusted to express, on the whole, the mind of his colleagues.

The Christian Revelation is what Reason by its own light (if permitted to shine clearly) might have foreseen. For it is simply the complete unveiling of the Divine goodness in view of man's spiritual need, and it is commensurate with the redeeming work of Christ. No doubt, Whichcote thought of all Scripture as somehow a revelation, but not a revelation of God or of the duties attaching to faith in God—except in the sense of clarifying and enforcing them. There is no hint of the modern view of the Old Testament as a record of the stages by which God progressively revealed Himself. On the other hand, he never quotes (like the Puritan) the Old Testament in a way which suggests that its examples of an inferior moral type, regarding God or man, carried any weight with him. His only use of it, as revelation, is in tracing the many and varied prophetic intimations of Christ which he seemed to find in certain characters and texts, and the sacrificial system. So, too, as to the New Testament, its doctrine of God or the moral law is not essentially an advance on that given by natural light. It does, indeed, clear and heighten this, but what it does, and was designed to do, is to demonstrate the fullness of Divine grace for man's salvation, here and hereafter. Its glory is the Cross. At the same time he works out no theory of atonement. He is content to say that it pleased God of His infinite goodness to send His Son that, by means of Him, forgiveness and a hope full of immortality should be assured to those who repent and believe in Him. Why this can have been necessary he does not presume to say. Certainly, the effect of Christ's work was to magnify God's righteousness; to add a deeper shade to the evil of sin; to suggest that forgiveness on God's part is not the easy thing it might appear to be, since it entailed so costly a sacrifice; and to melt the stony heart by a proof so gracious and undeserved of Divine Love. Reason can see all this and approve it all; and this perhaps is all that needs to be known. Anyhow, of one fact Whichcote is absolutely sure: that no view of the matter which ascribes to Christ more love to man than that of God, or makes him an object of God's wrath, or explains his sufferings as, in any sense or degree, penal, is deserving of the least respect. With his eye on those who maintained some such view, and called it orthodox, he is never tired of insisting that the whole transaction, from first to last, was motived by God's spontaneous love, and must be taken for a transcendent illustration of His goodness. Nor must the bounds and benefits of such grace be narrowed in any way. The offer of them is extended to all alike, and on the same simple terms of faith and repentance.

"Our welfare primarily and originally begins at God. God Himself, moved by His own goodness, doth entertain thoughts and purposes of good towards us." Let us be careful, therefore, "that we do not upon the occasion of our Saviour's interposing, or appearing, on our behalf, overlook the goodness of God, which was the first move towards our happiness, welfare and recovery." "Let us not upon that occasion—the great relief we have in the undertaking of the Son—at all prejudice, or derogate from, the primary, original and antecedent goodness of God. If we do, we do not observe Scripture: for wherever Christ is spoken of, God is acknowledged in the first place. God so loved the world that He gave His only begotten Son, etc., God in Christ reconciling the world unto Himself, etc., and He is made to us of God, wisdom, righteousness, sanctification and redemption. And observe our Saviour's expression upon all occasions: He says He seeks not His own honour but the honour of the Father. And how oft doth He declare that He was sent of God; that He came to do the will of God; and that He works that work wherein His Father had been before engaged." So if we "derogate from the original, primary goodness of God, we do not follow our Saviour's direction." "Wherefore, though it be a tender point, let us so satisfy ourselves concerning that expression of Christ's satisfaction for sin, as not at all to derogate from, or abate, God's free pardon of sin. The free pardon of sin to them that do repent, it is primarily and originally owing to the goodness of God Himself: though it is also to be attributed and ascribed to the interposing of our Lord and Saviour " as " *a secondary and a further promoting cause, and that which Divine wisdom did think fit should be,* but the original goodness of God is the primary cause of all." (ii. p. 100.)

The words I have italicised seem to disclose an inconsistency or even a contradiction. For if it be true—as Whichcote repeatedly asserts—that God has always been moved to forgive the penitent by His own goodness, what need of Christ as "a secondary and a further promoting cause"? Surely all He did, or needed to do, was to declare forgiveness to the penitent in a more public and impressive way than had been done before?—and Whichcote did not really mean more than this. But, for once, he was the victim of a metaphor —a metaphor which led him to use language descriptive of Christ as a third party eliciting a fullness of compassion which otherwise God would not have felt, and so working a change in God. What he meant was, I think, expressed in his use of the word "satisfaction." Thinking of Christ as at once Son of God and Son of Man, he says that as man's representative, Christ yielded God satisfaction, and thereby, as it were, made it easier—nay, more reasonable—for Him to proclaim a universal pardon. For Christ offered to God, on man's behalf, "His own sacrifice, which was an act of the most entire resignation in the world." He made Himself "a nothing." Thus "he obliterated man's presumption." He reversed com-

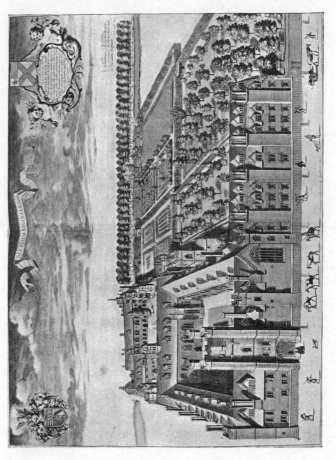

QUEENS' COLLEGE, CAMBRIDGE
From a print by David Loggan.

pletely "the first apostasy." He presented the "clean contrary." He rendered "such an acknowledgment to God as a fuller cannot be." He introduced a "new law of obedience, of the creature to the Creator." So, at the same time, He exposed the "quality of sin"; "its odiousness to God"; "its hurtfulness to man"; its just condemnation. He vindicated the righteousness of God in all His laws. He exalted God as "supreme and sovereign." And all this He did of His own free will. What "makes the sacrifice of Christ so transcending above the death of ten thousands of beasts, was because all these were merely passive; and Our Saviour did understand and mean all those noble ends."

We may discern here the profoundly true thought that Christ by His perfect moral obedience both satisfied God on men's behalf and justified God to the conscience of men. Thus He might be said to clear the way for the free expression of God's saving grace. And if Whichcote chose to describe this, in forensic language, as supplying God with an external impulse which further inclined Him "toward benignity, mercy, compassion, patience and forgiveness," we need not suppose that he meant more than this.

Nearly the whole of Whichcote's teaching on this subject is contained in the sermons on 2 Tim. i., 9, 10; and Hebrews ii. 17—and from these, mostly, the quotations have been drawn.

We may compare for a virtually equivalent view, in John Smith, the appendix to his "Discourse of Legal and Evangelical Righteousness." "The whole business of Christ" (he says) is to give "full and evident assurance"

F

to the world "that God doth indeed 'seek the saving of that which is lost.'"

1. Christ the Son of God, by partaking "every way of human nature" and carrying it through "infirmities and sufferings to eternal glory," shows "that God had not cast off human nature, but had a real mind to exalt and dignify it again."

2. So, too, Christ shows "what human nature may attain to, and how it may by humility, self-denial, Divine love, and a Christ-like life, rise above all visible heavens into a state of immortal glory and bliss."

3. And in this there was a manifestation of love on God's part, "enough to thaw all the icyness of men's hearts which self-love had quite frozen up"—considering how, in order to effect its end, Christ had to lay down His life "and thereby make propitiation and atonement for sin." But *how* He did this, Smith (like Whichcote) does not attempt to say.

4. Thus Christ awakens the conscience not merely to a sense of "sin and guilt," but also quiets it before "God's majesty and greatness" in the presentation of a mediator, through whom the penitent "may address himself to God without jealousy or doubting."

He adds a touch which is not quite congruous with the Christian thought of God, and is, I think, absent from Whichcote—"The Platonists wisely observed that between the pure Divinity and impure sinners, as there is no union, so no communion: it is very agreeable every way, and upon all accounts, that they who in themselves are altogether unworthy and under demerit, should come to God by a mediator."

There is not much in Henry More, and still less in Ralph Cudworth, on the atoning work of Christ—not because they assigned less importance to it than Whichcote and Smith, but because it lay outside the scope of what they wrote upon. About the clearest brief reference to the subject in More is the following (from his *Mystery of Godliness*, Book I. cap. 5, § 4): ". . . Compassion was in the Deity towards mankind, before the Incarnation and death of Christ. But the formal Declaration and visible Consignation of this Reconcilement was by Christ, according as He is revealed in the Gospel, Whose transactions on our behalf are nothing else but a *sweet and kind condescension of the Wisdom of God* . . . accommodating himself to our Humane Capacities and Properties to win us off, in a kindly way, to *Love* and *Obedience.*"

§ 3. THE USE OF REASON IN RELIGION

Ten controverted Terms explained

There are ten words which all belong to the self-same state and "differ but notionally or gradually, or as to our apprehension only." They are these: *Regeneration, conversion, adoption, vocation, sanctification, justification, reconciliation, redemption, salvation, glorification.*

"To stand upon nice or accurate distinction of them is superfluous, needless and useless; since Scripture uses them indifferently. But if you speak accurately I will tell you the import of them. *Regeneration* is used to distinguish the Divine heavenly life from the natural and animal. *Conversion*, that imports a run-a-gate one that had departed from God and righteousness; and he is now reduced from the practice of iniquity to his duty to God. *Adoption*, that intimates that a man both broke with God and parted from Him; and here is again the renewal of the former relation to God: he is again made the Son of God. *Vocation*, that imports the taking a man off from the ill usage and guise of the world. *Sanctification*, that imports the renewal of us in the spirit of our minds. *Justification* imports pardon of sin. *Redemption* imports rescuing us from the slavery of the devil. *Salvation*, holiness here, and happiness hereafter. *Reconciliation* implies peace restored with God, and with our consciences. *Glorification* is a consummation and accomplishment of them all." So "whensoever one of these is, all are . . . they speak the same thing in different states." "And this it is fit for you to know to avoid a troublesome multiplicity in religion and the possessing the minds of men with thoughts that religion is a more voluminous and intricate thing than indeed it is. . . . Can you discern one of these in yourselves, you may satisfy yourselves of all the rest: for truth lies in a narrow room, and little compass."—*Sermons*, vol. ii. pp. 80–82.

This is the preacher's way of touching off a subject, and it would not please some of the "learned scholars" he speaks of; but it must have brought great mental relief to many of his simpler hearers.

Heaven and Hell

"It is not possible for a man to be made happy by putting him into a *happy place*, unless he be in a good state. A man is not happy in the state wherein he is not qualified. We are not capable of happiness unless we be restored to innocency by repentance and renewed in part. The Gospel is the restitution of us to the state of our creation, to the use of our principles, to our healthful constitution, and to acts connatural to us." —Vol. iii. p. 95.

"There is no danger from God, if men be harmless and not self-condemned. The judgment of God at the last will be easy: for there will be none to be condemned but what were condemned before. For man's misery and harm doth not proceed from abroad, but arises out of himself, and is not by *positive infliction*. Men run upon mistakes: the wicked and profane think that if God *would*, they might take liberty to gratify and please themselves, and no harm done; and that it is the *will* of God only, that limits and restrains them; and they think that they were out of danger, if God would forbear a positive infliction; and that hell is only an incommodious place, that God by His power throws them into. This is the grand mistake. Hell is not only a positive infliction; neither is it possible that any man should be so miserable as the hellish state makes him, by any outward place only, but by the misery that ariseth out of his own self. For if omnipotency should load me with all burdens; if I were whole in myself, I could bear them, but if I be *faulty* and *guilty*, then I have a wound within me, and *I have nothing in myself, that is true to myself*. The fewel of *Tophet* burning is the guiltiness of man's conscience, malignity, and a naughty disposition against goodness and holiness; and God's withdrawing because the person is incapable of His communication. Sin is an act of violence in itself: the sinner doth force himself, and stirs up strife within himself; and in a sinner there is that *within* which doth reluctate, and condemn him in the inward court of his own conscience. For if our hearts condemn us not, all without might be avoided."—Vol. iii. 153.

The Wrath of God

" It is truly evangelical and apostolical, as well to declare the *wrath of God* against those that continue in sin, as to hold forth the grace and goodness of God towards those that do repent and believe . . . the Gospel privileges are not to give protection to sinners; but are cities of refuge for penitents."—Vol. iii. 156, 7.

Zeal, True and False

" It hath been long observed, that faction and mistaken zeal are a kind of *wild-fire*. The more false anyone is in his religion, the more fierce and furious: the more mistaken, the more imposing. The more any man's religion is his *own*, the more he is concerned for it, but cool and indifferent enough for that which is God's." —Vol. i. 166.

" To live in regard of God; to deal fairly and equally and righteously with our neighbour; and soberly and temperately as to ourselves; and wheresoever a man fails, to return by repentance and go to God for pardon in the name of the Lord Jesus: I could wish that the world would but consent that *these four* might be the materials of religion. These matters have general consent, but great neglect. And instead of zeal for these, wherein have men's zeal been exercised, but about certain usages, certain modes, and rites of parties? By these men are constituted and denominated Christians, and ranked in order and file. Here is the miscarriage. This I account the greatest folly and madness in the world. It is recorded that the strifes and contentions and complaints of Christians have irritated some of the ten heathenish persecutions. The ill lives of Christians and their absurd opinions, and the bestowing their zeal upon matters wherein parties are constituted, have kept nations off from becoming Christian. These things have been the scandal of Christianity."—Vol. iii. 252.

"I will not contradict the reason of my mind, either by temper or practice. I will allow myself in no known unrighteousness, but will be as good as I ought to be, and will pursue my judgment by practice. But as to others, I have nothing to do with them (if I be a private person) but by reason and argument; and to show a great deal of patience and meekness, and gentleness of spirit; repeat (this) again and again: if truth be not admitted one day, it may be another. Let me be such as the doctrine of the Gospel declares I ought to be, and then by my example I shall promote the truth. If we were but rid of our several mistakes and superstitions, and nothing left but what is sound religion, we should be cool enough. For the greatest zeal is in things doubtful and questionable; but things unquestionable—as entire resignation to God, humility and modesty, meekness, gentleness, etc.—there is no great zeal in the world about these. Now these things exceed all."—Vol. ii. 261.

Scripture

"If you let go Scripture in the sense to which the context leads, and if you let go the true and impartial proposals and dictates of sober reason, then do we open the door to all manner of delusion and imposture, and shall be carried we know not whither. Let us stand by these two; for these are the two certain principles. If we lay these aside, we do not know where we shall be carried, unless we fall into the hands of truly divinely inspired men."—Vol. iii. 117.

"In the Bible there are these two things: the consonancy of the things therein contained with the things of natural knowledge, and the report there made of God, agreeable to what reason leads men to think." —Ibid. 191.

". . . Scripture as it is a matter of faith, is not a single text, but all the Scripture; and not so much the words as the sense, that sense which is verified by other scriptures. For you may take it for granted, that there is no matter of faith, or duty, that stands upon the authority of one single text; and that sense which is not otherwise, is nowhere to be taken. . . . God expects that the reader of Scripture should be of an ingenuous spirit, and use candor, and not lie at the catch: for the Scripture is to be read as a man would read a letter from a friend, in which he doth only look after what was his friend's mind and meaning, not what he can put upon the words."—Vol. ii. 245.

Reason requires that we think the best of God

" . . . We do not disparage the Almighty, or cast limitations upon omnipotency itself, to say, upon supposition of one thing, that another must necessarily follow. As, for instance, if God makes a promise, He must perform it; if He makes a creature intelligent and voluntary, He must use him as such; if the creature He hath made be finite and fallible, He must give him allowance." This stands to reason, and has the support of Scripture (Isa. i. 18; v. 3; xlvi. 8). " 'Tis well resolved by one, that it was not so much boldly as worthily spoken by him that said: *There is that in God that is more beautiful than power, than will and Sovereignty, viz. His righteousness, His good-will, His justice, wisdom and the like."*— Vol. ii. 244.

The Gospel

"The doctrine of the Gospel is no invention of human reason. Man did not prevent God by any thought of it beforehand, or any desire. Man merited it not at God's hands, neither hath after recompensed it. Only the necessity of man's state required it, and God's goodness afforded it. 'Tis persuasive and affecting in the strongest way of motive and argument, which are proper ways of acting in the intellectual world. The excellency of infinite wisdom, power, and goodness is displayed in it, and God, by it, works powerfully in us, and upon us: and this commanding is in the highest way of reason. No better way of arguing than by strong reason and convincing argument; and no such conviction, no fuller satisfaction, in any undertaking, than in the business of regeneration and conversion."—Vol. iii. 86.

God in Christ

" . . . What more satisfaction can there be to the reason of our minds, what more tending to the quiet of our conscience, than to be assured, in a matter of such importance to us, that God, to whom we are so liable and obnoxious by transgression and sin, is the most lovely, placable and reconcilable being, of Himself, through the perfection of His own nature; and that in the grace of the Gospel, He is absolutely resolved and engaged, by His voluntary determination and promise to pardon sin, in and through Christ, to all who repent and believe the Gospel? And this, and nothing less than this, is the matter of the Gospel. This is *to be accepted in and through Christ*; this is the true explication—God in, and through Christ, will pardon sin to all that leave off sin, and ask Him forgiveness, and return to duty. This is the true explication of *Justification by imputed righteousness*; and whatsoever is beyond this is imaginary, and will deceive any man."—Vol. iii. 75.

The Effects of true Religion

" . . . Give me religion that is grounded in reason and by divine authority; and that doth attain real effects, such as are worthy what we mean by religion.

In short, to instance in particulars: the religion that makes men humble and modest, not proud and conceited; that makes men poor in Spirit, not full of their own mind, not grown up to their own sense, and thereupon to self-will; the religion that makes men good-natured, not all for themselves; that makes them loving, and not hard-hearted; that makes men kind, not harsh and cruel; . . . the religion that makes men subject and obedient to government and authority, not that that is turbulent and troublesome; the religion that makes men courteous, affable and sociable, not sour, morose, and dogged; that makes men ready to forgive, not implacable; the religion that makes men favourable in making best constructions of words, carriages, and behaviour, and not that that makes *men offended for a word*, as the prophet speaks (Isa. xxix. 21) . . . the religion that makes men ready to commiserate in every compassionable case, as God does, Samaritan - like, tender-hearted—not as the Jews that would have no dealings or converse but with those of their own nation, unless they agreed with them in all their modes. This is what religion is in its proper effects, and if this religion took place in the world, then shall the world be sensible of the good of religion, and we should all find ourselves the better for it."—Vol. iii. 271, 272.

"An uncharitable Christianity, unmerciful, void of good-nature, is no more religion than a *dark sun* is a sun, or a *cold fire* is fire. He only can dwell in God who dwells in love. . . . To be out of love and good-will, is to be in the devil's form and spirit."—Vol. iii. 332.

'Tis in Ourselves that we are Thus and Thus

"We are very apt to lay all the fault upon our natures; but really our wills are rather to be blamed. That that undoes us, is our perverse wills, corrupt affections, stubborn hearts; and these do more harm in the world than weak heads: 'tis not so much want of knowledge as goodness. God is a great deal more known in the world than He is either observed or loved. But this will be the world's condemnation, that where men either did know and might know, there they either grossly neglected themselves, or went against their light; that men put out the candle of God's spirit in them, that they may do evil without check or control; that men take upon them to control the settled and immutable laws of everlasting righteousness, goodness and truth, which is the law of heaven; that men are bold to confound order and government in God's family (for so the world is); that men do evil *knowingly* in the abuse of their liberty and freedom; whereas God Himself, in whom there is the fulness of all liberty, doth declare of Himself, that all His ways are ways of *goodness, righteousness* and *truth*. And can God by power or privilege do that which is not fit and just? Is there any unrighteousness with God? God forbid. Yet creatures that are of limited powers, and have liberty by participation only, pretending the use of liberty, extend liberty beyond the bounds of law, and do that which is not fit to be done. This is the world's condemnation."—Vol. iii. 152.

God the Mind's chief Employment

"It is the proper employment of our intellectual faculties to be conversant about God, to conceive aright of Him; and then to resemble and imitate Him. Religion is an obligation upon us to God; the *first* motion of religion is to understand what is true of God; and the *second* is to express it in our lives, and to copy it out in our works. The *former* is our wisdom, and the *latter* is our goodness. In these two consist the health and pulchritude of our minds. For health to the body is not more than virtue is to the mind. A depraved and vicious mind is as really the sickness and deformity thereof, as any foul and loathsome disease is to the body. And as really as these tend to the death and dissolution of the soul and body, so the vices of the mind tend to the separation of God and the soul."—Ibid. 100.

Without God

"The mind diverted from God wanders in darkness and confusion. But being directed to Him, soon finds its way, and doth receive from Him in a way that is abstracted from the noise of the world, and withdrawn from the call of the body; having shut the doors of our senses, to recommend ourselves to the Divine light, which readily enters into the eye of the mind that is prepared to receive it. For there is light enough of God in the world, if the eye of our minds were but fitted to receive it, and let it in. It is the incapacity of the subject, where God is not; for nothing in the world is more knowable than God. God only is absent to them that are indisposed and disaffected. For a man cannot open his eye, nor lend his ear, but everything will declare more or less of God. It is our fault that we are estranged from Him: for God doth not withdraw Himself from us, unless we first leave Him; the distance is occasioned through our unnatural use of ourselves."—Vol. iii. 102.

Excuse for Sin

". . . Three things put together do something to lessen the sins of man and procure him pity with God. (1) That he is liable to fail and be mistaken. (2) That in his constitution he doth consist of body and spirit; and (3) that he is exposed to all sorts of temptations from without, in this dangerous and hazardous world." Hence, being what he is, God might be expected to manifest His compassion. The gift of His Son to save man and restore him to his lost estate, *became* him, i.e. was in keeping with his character and the facts of the case. "So that through the grace of God it is not so much what sin is, as what the demeanour of a person is, after sin. Therefore, these two cases differ extremely: a sinner that is awakened and considerate, that *leaves off to sin,* that deprecates God's displeasure, and asks His forgiveness and returns to his duty, that importunes God for mercy, and follows God's directions, this man's case is compassionable." But "a sinner that *still goes on in a way of wickedness,* and hardens his heart against God"—his case is very different; and the "very self-same goodness that inclines God to pardon the former, requires Him to condemn the latter. The same goodness that doth pardon penitents, doth punish obstinacy."—Vol. ii. 251.

Real Sinners

". . . All that in any Scripture are branded for
sinners . . . are men that sin against their knowledge,
imprison the truth of God, and hold it in unrighteousness.
I call these sinners that the Scripture doth. I find in the
language of Scripture, none are nominated sinners but
such" as these. "The Scripture doth never fasten the title
or denomination upon them that mean well, but are in
something mistaken; who now and then are under an
error, having failings, imperfections, and shortnesses;
that do now and then miscarry upon a violent temptation
or sudden surprisal. You never find these men are called
sinners; neither are the infirmities of the regenerate, the
sincere and upright-hearted called sins. . . . These things
do befall the best of us at times; but after awhile we recover ourselves, and then ask God forgiveness, and make
use of faith for expiation in Christ's blood; we pray God
for grace to recover us and for more strength for the
time to come. These are sins that require God's forgiveness, and are a true cause for us to be humble, and
modest, and to depend upon God—but they do not break
our peace with God, neither do they havoc conscience,
or denominate a man a *sinner*."—Vol. iii. 135, 136.

The Peace of Repentance

"Wherefore, O man, whosoever thou art who sufferest,
wouldest thou effectually ease thy condition? I advise
thee to these two things: put thyself upon self-examina-
tion, and the motion of repentance. The motion of
repentance will quite alter the case, and all the world

cannot give thee heart's ease, save in this way. For
this is the greatest Gospel-grace, that repentance should
prove effectual; that it should be otherwise with a sinner
that repents, than with a sinner that doth not repent:
for where we condemn ourselves, God will forbear. Upon
a moral consideration a man is not the same: for, after
repentance, the man is passed into another spirit, and
there is another law of his life. I daresay without repentance, a sinner could not be eased in his own mind. If he
have offered force to himself, in respect of his own
principles, he cannot have content in his own mind,
tho' God should withdraw and take his own hand off.
There is no possibility of ease to a guilty conscience,
unless a man do repent."—Vol. iii. 233.

CHAPTER III

JOHN SMITH (1616–1652)

THE bearer of this common name was perhaps the most uncommon of the little band with whom we are dealing. This was recognised by his fellows at Cambridge and is amply proved by his *Select Discourses*. Few men can ever have made so deep an impression of greatness on pupils and friends, or have inspired so profound an affection. Nor is there anything in the writings of the Cambridge men so irresistibly suggestive of intellectual and spiritual genius as his *Discourses*.

He came of humble stock. His parents, John and Catherine Smith, belonged to the respectable poor who pass their days in many a country spot. Their place of life and death was one of the smallest villages of North-amptonshire—Achurch on the Nene, an affluent of the Ouse; and within sight of Aldwinkle, birthplace of the poet Dryden.

He was born—like John the Baptist—"after his parents had been long childless and were grown aged." [1] "Some have observed," says his eulogist Patrick, "that such (children) have proved very famous," and "are something like Isaac who had a great blessing in him; and seem to be intended by God for some great service and work in the world." We learn from the Parish

[1] His father had been chosen a churchwarden as early as November 1601.

Register that his mother was buried on 4 April, 1616—a few months after his birth. (How long his father survived her is not known.) He was not baptised till 15 February, 1618—a circumstance which may account for the usual statement that he was born in 1618. Three miles from Achurch is the little market town of Oundle with a fine Grammar School—founded in the second half of the sixteenth century. Here probably he began his regular education. His studious bent showed itself at once. "He shook off all idleness and sloth, the bane of youth; and so had the blessings of God upon his endeavours, Who gave him great encouragement from divers persons of worth." The reference here is to local benefactors by whom he was assisted to Cambridge, where he entered as a pensioner [1] at Emmanuel College on 5 April, 1636. The choice of Emmanuel may imply Puritan leanings on the part of his parents, but perhaps a more decisive Puritan influence was that of the rector—the notorious Robert Brown who held the living from January 1592 to May 1631. True, this pioneer of the advanced Puritanism known as Independency had conformed; but there is reason to believe that conformity in his case did not mean conversion. True, also, he appears to have been non-resident in Achurch from September 1619 to June 1626, but this would still allow of contact with Smith during the ten most impressionable years of his youth. Anyhow, it may be accepted as certain that, while Brown's influence might not be commended by his

---

[1] So Mullinger in *D.N.B.*, but Venn, in *Alumni Cantabrigienses* (1922), says "Sizar," a term at Cambridge answering to "Servitor" at Oxford. "The name probably indicates that the person so designated received his sizes free, i.e. allowances of bread, ale, etc."—*Oxford Dictionary*.

character, what there was of it went to strengthen Puritan sentiment in the parish generally, and so in the home of Smith, even apart from much personal intercourse.

How far the generous friends who enabled him to pay for his commons and other expenses when he first came up to the University continued to help him, we do not know; but, if they fell off, he found a no less effectual friend in his tutor, Benjamin Whichcote, for whom he at once conceived "a great and singular regard." The regard soon became mutual; and, while the young student valued most of all those "directions and encouragements" in his studies which "his careful tutor" bestowed so readily upon one whom he esteemed "for his excellent improvements in the choicest parts of learning," he did not refuse "the reasonable support and maintenance" which Whichcote could well afford to give, and knew how to give with delicate kindness. In this way, his first years at Cambridge were set free from anxiety; and, for the rest, "his great industry and indefatigable pains, his Herculean labours day and night" speedily raised him to a position of independence. Yet, strange to say, it took him eight years to complete his graduation—a fact due, one imagines, to breakdowns of health, consequent on excessive study. He proceeded B.A. in 1640 and M.A. in 1644. The delay cost him his chance of an Emmanuel Fellowship. For, by a statute of the college then in force, there could not be more than one Fellow from the same county at the same time; and, as William Dillingham (1617?–1689), also a native of Northamptonshire, had been made Fellow on 19 November, 1642, Smith was barred out. But on 11 April,

1644, he was one of nine nominees whom the Earl of Manchester, acting for Parliament, appointed to Fellowships at Queens' College.[1] In the same year he became Hebrew Lecturer and Censor Philosophicus—to which offices was added in the year following, that of Greek Prælector. He lectured also in Mathematics.[2] His work for the next few years was chiefly that of a tutor—in which he achieved rare success. Then in 1650 he became Dean and Catechist of his college; in which capacity—during his year of office—he was expected to preach a certain number of times in the college chapel; and here he delivered the bulk of those ten *Discourses* by which he is known.

But not the whole of them. For, by the time he had finished the sixth his term of office ran out, and, not long after, "those bodily distempers and weaknesses began more violently to seize upon him which the summer following put a period to his life." [3] He died on 7 August, 1652. For many weeks before the end he suffered greatly, but "passed the last six days of his life . . . in a kind of sleep." His interment took place in an unmarked spot of the college chapel; and was attended by the Vice-Chancellor of the University, all the Heads of Houses, and many others. A Senior Fellow of Queens', Simon

[1] They were first examined and approved by the Assembly of Divines, then sitting at Westminster.

[2] Although it is doubtful whether this implied anything more than arithmetic.

[3] "I have sometimes told you of Mr. Smith, of Queens' College, a person of such eminency in religion and in ingenuous learning. I question whether we shall long enjoy him in this world. He hath for some two years been troubled with a cough and I fear hath studied himself into a consumption. He is now in London consulting with doctors to see if there be hope. Yours, I. W. April 6, 1652."—Letter sent to Mr. S. H., quoted by Mullinger, iii. 631, n.

Patrick—afterwards Bishop of Ely—preached on the occasion and the very extravagance of his eulogy, spoken before such an audience, served but to emphasise the unique place Smith had won in their reverent affection.[1] Patrick dwells on his intellectual, but mainly on his spiritual, qualities. In learning he could do what he would. "He had such a huge, wide capacity of soul, such a sharp and piercing understanding, such a deep searching mind that he set himself about nothing but he soon grasped it, and made himself a full possessor of it." Thus he became a "living library," a compendium of the six hundred books which he left to the college. But he was not a "library locked up nor a book clasped." On the contrary, he "stood open for any to converse withal that had a mind to learn. Yea, he was a Fountain running over, labouring to do good to those who perhaps had no mind to receive it. None more free and communicative than he was, to such as desired to discourse with him; nor would he grudge to be taken off from his studies upon such an occasion."

In a word, he was not a pedant. He did not prize learning merely for its own sake. He made it an instrument of service. He practised the lesson, freely ye have received, freely give; and herein appeared what, to all who knew him, was his chief excellence, viz. an unfeigned humility. "From his first admission into the University he sought not great things for himself, but

[1] The text was 2 Kings ii. 13. It seems to have been suggested by the oration of Gregory of Nyssa on his brother Basil from the same text. Richard Baxter's funeral sermon by Matthew Sylvester in 1691 was based on the same passage. This sermon, together with Worthington's Preface to the *Discourses* and a few references in the latter's *Diary*, are the scant sources of all that is known about him.

was contented in the condition wherein he was. He made not haste to rise and climb, as youths are apt to do . . . but proceeded leisurely, by orderly steps, not to what he could get, but to what he was fit to undertake. He staid God's time of advancement, with all industry and pains following his studies; as if he rather desired to deserve honour than to be honoured."

No one, it is said, "ever beheld in him any pride, vainglory, boasting, self-conceit, desire of honour and being famous in the world." He was eminently "a true Disciple of Jesus Christ who took upon Him the form of a servant, and made Himself of no reputation." "And I daresay," says Patrick, "our dear friend was as true, as humble a servant . . . to the good of mankind as any person that this day lives. This was his design in his studies; and if it had pleased the Lord of Life to have prolonged his days it would have been more of his work: for he was resolved (as he once told me) very much to lay aside other studies, and to travel (travail) in the Salvation of men's souls, after whose good he most ardently thirsted." Another conspicuous trait was his sweetness and graciousness—"the more remarkable," it is said, "because he was of a temper naturally hot and choleric, as the greatest minds most commonly are." He was seldom stirred to anger, and never by the occasions which excite most men's anger. His anger was reserved for something really wicked; and even then "was but a sudden flushing of the face" which "did as soon vanish as arise." In fine, his habitual state was one of "great serenity, quiet and tranquillity." He "dwelt so much above that his soul was not shaken with any of those tempests and storms which use to un-

settle more low and abject minds." "He lived in a continued sweet enjoyment of God."

And it is important to remark that with all his devoted-
ness and indebtedness to teachers like Plato and Plotinus,
the place he gave to Christ was supreme. Christ in his
experience was more than a Teacher. He was a Saviour.
Patrick speaks of "his true, lively and working Faith,
his simple, plain-hearted, naked Faith in Christ" as the
root and mainspring of his spiritual life. It was a faith
which "did not busy itself about many fine notions,
subtleties and curiosities, or believing whole volumes;
but . . . was firmly set and fixed in the mercy and
goodness of God through Christ." It was such a faith as
"brought down Christ into his soul" and "made him
hearty, serious and constant" in all Christian virtues.
"It made him god-like," and "truly partaker of the
Righteousness of Christ." "All that remember the serious
behaviour and weighty expressions he used in his prayers,
cannot but call to mind how much his heart was set upon
the attainment of this true goodness." Such was John
Smith as seen through the eyes of friends who stood
nearest to him; and, in no small degree, their impression
is borne out by his *Select Discourses*. The range and
variety of the knowledge these indicate is amazing,
so is their style, which—in the marks of a stately yet
easy eloquence—it would be hard to match; so is their
wealth and depth of thought; so, in particular, is their
elevation and spiritual glow, which bespeak, if not
exactly the mystic, yet the man at home with the
things of God.

As already said, they are ten in number. The first
edition appeared in 1660—eight years after the preacher's

death, the delay being partly accounted for by the immense difficulties which Dr. Worthington, the editor, encountered in arranging them.[1] A second edition—almost an exact reprint of the first—came out in 1678; a third in 1821; and a fourth—the Editio optime—corrected and revised for the Syndics of the Cambridge University Press by Henry Griffin Williams, B.D., in 1859. Besides these complete editions, extracted portions were printed by John Wesley in his "Christian Library" (1749) — portions covering 100 pages of Vols. xix., xx. Wesley adds a P.S. to say that he is "sensible some parts of the following discourses are scarce intelligible to unlearned readers," but that he "could not prevail with himself, on that account, to rob those who can understand them of so great a treasure." Another abridgment was made by Lord Hailes and published in 1756; and still another by John King, M.A. of Queens' College, Cambridge, in 1820. Dr. Watson, Bishop of Llandaff (1737–1816), issued the Discourse of Prophecy" in a *Collection of Theological Tracts*, 1785: and Le Clerc inserted a translation of the same in his *Vetus Testamentum* (1710–1731). The Discourse on "The Excellency and Nobleness of True Religion" was also issued separately by a Glasgow publisher, Robert Fontis, in 1745, and by a London publisher, Emily Faithful, in 1864. Metcalfe's volume of Selections (1882)—under the title, *Natural Truth of Christianity*, which reached a second edition in 1885—is fairly well known. Smith, it thus appears, has been somewhat more popular than his fellows. It is interesting

---

[1] They had come to his hands from Smith's executor, Samuel Cradock, in a chaotic state.

to note in this connection, that Dr. John Howe (1630–1705), whose spacious and luminous mind marks him off from most of his nonconformist contemporaries, is said to have derived his "Platonic Tincture" mainly from Smith; and that S. T. Coleridge (1772–1834), at a much later date, was one of his admiring readers. He quotes him in *Aids to Reflection* (Vol. i. 199), and comments upon him in his *Literary Remains*.

Moreover, his copy of a first edition of the *Select Discourses*—which is still extant and till lately was in the possession of Mr. J. Finlayson, Victoria Park, Manchester (1888)—has "its margins and blank pages" scrawled with the Poet-Philosopher's autograph notes. Also, the late Alexander Knox (1757–1831) was strongly attracted by Smith, and declared, "My value for him is beyond what words can express."

And Matthew Arnold's (1828–1888) appreciation, prefixed to Metcalfe's "Selections," closes with these words:

"I have often thought that if candidates for holy orders were simply, in preparing for their examination, to read and digest Smith's great discourse on *The Excellency and Nobleness of True Religion*, together with M. Reuss's *History of Christian Theology at the Time of the Apostles*, and nothing further except the Bible itself, we might have, perhaps, a hope of at last getting, as our national guides in religion, a clergy which could tell its bearings and steer its way, instead of being, as we now see it, too often conspicuously at a loss to do either."

Smith used to say that he "lived on Dr. Whichcote"; and meant by this that his mind found the thoughts of his teacher congenial and nourishing to a high degree.

Hence his own discourses might be expected to re-produce the teacher's thoughts; and they do. Everything said by Whichcote was re-said by Smith; but not slavishly. The pupil first of all had made it his own, and brought it to the touchstone of his own experience, and confirmed it by the testimony of others, and enriched its contents from the Fathers, or the Platonists. Further, his emphasis was different. He valued, as much as Whichcote, the natural evidences of religious and moral truth; its foundation in man's reason; its necessary relatedness to a "godly, righteous and sober life." But he dwelt more on the inwardness of religion, on the spirit of Christ as the living spring of Evangelical righteousness, on the mystic union with God which is the effect of obedience, and is the surest pledge of immortality.

From this standpoint, there is nothing more characteristic of Smith than the first of the Discourses—the one "Concerning the True Way or Method of attaining Divine Knowledge." It says in brief what is expressed under various aspects in the rest. It is the epitome of his mind. If, therefore, I keep mainly to this I shall be carrying out my purpose to mark off each of the Cambridge men by his most distinguishing feature. But by way of introduction I will quote a passage from the Discourse on "The Excellency and Nobleness of True Religion," to show his general agreement with Whichcote.

1. "Reason in man being *lumen de lumine*, a light flowing from the fountain and father of lights . . . it was to enable man to work out of himself all those notions of God which are the true Groundwork of Love and Obedience to God and conformity to Him; and, in

moulding the inward man into the greatest conformity
to the nature of God, was the Perfection and Efficacy
of the Religion of Nature.

2. "But since Man's fall from God, the inward virtue
and vigour of Reason is much abated . . . those principles
of Divine truth which were first engraven upon man's
heart with the finger of God are now, as the Characters
of some ancient monuments, less clear and legible than
at first.

3. "Therefore, besides the truth of natural inscription, God hath provided the truth of Divine revelation
which issues forth from His own free will, and clearly
discovers the way of our return to God from Whom we
have fallen. And *this* truth, with the effects and pro-
ductions of it in the minds of men, the Scripture is wont
to set forth under the name of *grace*, as proceeding
merely from the free bounty and overflowings of the
Divine love. . . . But, besides this *outward* revelation of
God's will to men, there is also an *inward* impression of
it on their minds and spirits, which is, in a more special
manner, attributed to God. *We cannot see Divine things
but in a Divine light:* God only, Who is the true light
and in Whom there is no darkness at all, can so shine
out of Himself upon our glassy understandings as to
beget in them a picture of Himself, His own will and
pleasure; and turn the soul, as the phrase is in Job . . .
'like wax or clay to the seal' of His own light and love.
. . . *Men may teach the grammar and rhetoric, but God
teaches the Divinity.* Thus it is God alone that acquaints
the soul with the truths of revelation: and He it is,
also, that does strengthen and raise the soul to better
apprehensions even of *natural* truth: 'God being that

in the intellectual world which the sun is in the sensible,'
as some of the ancient fathers love to speak, and the
ancient philosophers too. . . ." (Chap. i.)

*We cannot see Divine things but in a Divine Light;
and our measure of Divine light is conditioned by our
advance in the Divine life*—this truth, heard at first
from Whichcote's lips, was that which took deepest
hold of Smith.

There are, he says—"setting aside the Epicurean
herd of brutish men, who have drowned all their own
sober reason in the deepest Lethe of sensuality "—four
different orders of men. There is (1) the "complex and
multifarious man " in whom " sense and reason are so
twisted together " that he gets no clear perception of
" first principles." His " highest reason is complying
with his senses and both conspire together in vulgar
opinion." The Stoic motto βίος ὑπόληψις applies to
him. His life is " steered by nothing else but opinion
and imagination." His "higher notions of God and
religion are so entangled with the birdlime of fleshly
passions and mundane vanity that" he "cannot rise up
above the surface of this dark earth, or easily entertain
any but earthly conceptions of heavenly things." "Such
souls are 'heavy behind,' [1] and are continually pressing
down to this world's centre."

There is (2) the Rationalist, or the man who "thinks
not fit to view his own face in any other glass but that
of reason and understanding." "In such a one the
communes notitiæ, or common principles of virtue and
goodness, are more clear and steady." But being unfed
and unfilled "with the practice of true virtue," they

[1] ὀπισθοβαρεῖς.

"may be but poor, empty, and hungry things of themselves."

There is (3) the Enthusiast, who has an "inward sense of virtue and moral goodness far transcendent to all mere speculative opinions of it"; but whose soul is apt, too much, to "heave and swell with the sense of" his "own virtue and knowledge." "An ill-ferment of self-love, lying at the bottom," frequently puffs up such a soul "with pride, arrogance and self-conceit."

Lastly, there is "the true metaphysical and contemplative man, . . . who running and shooting up above his own logical or self-rational life, pierceth into the highest life." Such a one "by universal love and holy affection, abstracting himself from himself, endeavours the nearest union with the Divine essence that may be . . . knitting his own centre, if he have any, into the centre of Divine being." [1] "To such a one the Platonists are wont to attribute a true Divine wisdom powerfully displaying itself in an 'intellectual life,' as they phrase it. Such a knowledge, they say, is always pregnant with Divine virtue, which ariseth out of a happy union of souls with God; and is nothing else but a living imitation of a God-like perfection—drawn out by a strong fervent love of it. This Divine knowledge . . . as Plotinus says, makes us amorous of divine beauty, beautiful and lovely; and this Divine love and purity reciprocally exalt Divine knowledge. . . . Though, by the Platonists' leave, such a life and knowledge as this is, peculiarly belongs to the true and sober Christian, who lives in Him who is life itself, and is enlightened by Him who is the truth itself, and is made partaker of the

[1] "As Plato says."

Divine unction, and 'knoweth all things,' as St. John speaks. This life is nothing else but God's own breath within him and an infant Christ (if I may use the expression) formed in his soul."

Whatever else he says, Smith always comes back to this, ends always on this note. You must do and be in order to know; you must act as if there were a God, as if the highest dictates of reason were the dictates of His will, as if obedience to these were the chief business of life, as if your purest desires and thoughts and hopes were in correspondence with an infinite fullness of Divine grace and truth—and acting thus, you will not be deceived; you will learn the "excellency and noble- ness of true Religion"; you will know all spiritual truth by a heat and radiancy of inward evidence surpassing the utmost cogency of logic.

For illustration, let me take what Smith, supporting himself on the Platonists and the Stoic philosophy, calls the first or fundamental principles of all religion—God and Immortality. As to the latter he is sure that the fact is demonstrable by Reason. Reflection on the soul itself is enough to demonstrate it.

"If we reflect but upon our own souls, how manifestly do the species of Reason, freedom, perception, and the like offer themselves to us, whereby we may know a thousand times more distinctly what our Souls are than what our Bodies are! For the former we know by an immediate converse with ourselves, and a distinct sense of their operations; whereas all our knowledge of the body is little better than merely historical, which we gather up by scraps and piecemeals from doubtful and uncertain experiments which we make of them: but the notions which we have of a mind, i.e. something within us that thinks, apprehends, reasons and discourses, are so clear and distinct from all those notions which we can fasten upon a body, that we can easily conceive that if all body-being in the world were destroyed, yet we might then as well subsist as we now do." [1]

The argument from self-consciousness against materialism could hardly be better put; and Smith himself thought much of it. But such an intellectual method of proof counted with him less than the moral. "Our highest speculations of the soul may beget a sufficient conviction thereof within us, but yet it is only true goodness and virtue in the souls of men that can make them both know and love, believe and delight themselves in their own immortality. Though every good man is not so logically subtle as to be able, by fit mediums, to demonstrate his own immortality, yet he *sees* it in a higher light. His soul, being purged and enlightened by true sanctity, is more capable of those Divine irradiations, whereby it feels itself in conjunction with God; and by the light of divine goodness, mixing itself with the light of its own reason, sees more clearly not only that it may, if it please the supreme Deity, of its own nature exist eternally, but also that it *shall* do so; it knows it shall never be deserted of that free goodness that always embraceth it: it knows *that* Almighty love, which it lives by, to be stronger than death, and more powerful than the grave; it will not suffer those holy ones that are partakers of it to lie in hell, or their souls to see corruption; and, though worms may devour their flesh, and putrefaction enter into

[1] "Discourse of the Immortality of the Soul." chap. vi.

those bones that fence it, yet it knows that its Redeemer lives and that it shall at last see Him with a pure intellectual eye, which will then be clear and bright, when all that earthly dust which converse with this earthly body filled it with, shall be removed: it knows that God will never forsake His own life which He hath quickened in it; He will never deny those ardent desires of a blissful fruition of Himself, which the lively sense of His own goodness hath excited within it: those breathings and gaspings after an eternal participation of Him are but the energy of His own breath within us. If He had any mind to destroy it, He would never have shown it such things as He hath done; He would not raise it up to such mounts of vision, to show it all the glory of that Canaan flowing with eternal and unbounded pleasures, and then precipitate it again into that deep and darkest abyss of death and non-entity. Divine goodness cannot, it will not, be so cruel to holy souls that are such ambitious suitors for His love." [1]

We remember how the saints of the Old Testament trod the same path to faith in a continuance of fullness of life hereafter; and we recall Henry More's lines:

> But souls that of his own good life partake
> He loves as His own self, dear as His eye
> They are to Him; He'll never them forsake.
> When they shall die, then God himself shall die:
> They live, they live in blest eternity.

Again, as to the existence and nature of God, Smith is sure that the sources of intellectual proof are clear—are, in fact, sufficiently laid in man's very being.

For God has so "copied forth Himself into the whole life and energy of man's soul as that the lovely characters

[1] "Discourse of the Immortality of the Soul," chap. vii.

of Divinity may be most easily seen and read by all men
within themselves: as they say Phidias the famous
statuary, after he had made the statue of Minerva,
with the greatest exquisiteness of Art, to be set up in
the Acropolis at Athens, afterwards impressed his own
image so deeply in her buckler that no one could delete
it without first reducing the whole statue to powder.
And if we would know what the *impresse* of souls is, it
is nothing but God Himself who could not write His
own name but only on rational natures." [1] Reason,
conscience, will, affection—all these aspects of the
human correspond to a God who has them all in perfection. As the Schoolmen said, Creation: the heavens
and the earth: bear the imprint of God's *feet*, but intelligible beings show forth His *face*.[2] And this men
would always have realised, but for the fact that sin has
intervened. It is sin alone which destroys capacity for
knowing God. Sin, therefore, must be done away if true
knowledge of God is to be restored. So, the return to
God is by a moral path. "It is not lawful for any impure
nature to touch divinity," said Socrates.

"We cannot enjoy God by any external conjunction
with Him. Divine fruition . . . is an internal (moral)
union—mediated, on God's side, by the strength of a
Divine life which He freely gives; and, on man's side,
by an integrity of heart which enables him freely to
receive."

"Sin, by its deadly infusions with the souls of men,
wastes and eats out the innate vigour of the soul . . .
but religion"—that is, the issue in man of a divine life,

[1] "Of the Existence and Nature of God," p. 134.
[2] Ibid., p. 136.

H

and his own corresponding obedience—"awakens and enlivens it, and makes it renew its strength like an eagle, and mount strongly upwards towards heaven; and so, uniting the soul to God, the centre of life and strength, it renders the soul undaunted and invincible."

So it is generally. The simplest yet the deepest rule for the true attainment—sooner or later—of all Divine knowledge and power is unqualified obedience.

In Smith's day there were two large classes of men whom he seems often to have had in mind.

1. There was the stolidly complacent Christian—sure of his acceptance with God, because sure of his ortho- doxy. Such a man had much to say, and said it unctuously, about Christ's work *for* him, about the blood of sprinkling, about His calling and election.

But Smith answers:

"God respects not a bold, confident, and audacious faith that is big with nothing but its own presumptions . . . it is not all our strong dreams of being in favour with heaven . . . it is not a pertinacious imagination of our names being enrolled in the book of life, or of the debt-books of heaven being crossed, or of Christ being ours . . . or of the washing away of our sins in His blood . . . it is not, I say, a pertinacious imagination of any of these that can make us the better: and a mere conceit or opinion, as it makes us never the better in reality within ourselves, so it cannot render us the more acceptable to God who judges of all things as they are." ("Discourse of Legal and Evangelical Righteous- ness," chap. v.)

"Far be it from me to disparage in the least the merit of Christ's blood, His becoming obedient unto death, whereby we are justified. But I doubt sometimes some of our dogmata and notions about Justification may puff us up in far higher and goodlier conceits of ourselves than God hath of us; and that we profanely make the unspotted righteousness of Christ to serve only as a covering wherein to wrap up our foul deformities and filthy vices; and when we have done, think ourselves in as good credit and repute with God as we are with ourselves; and that we are become heaven's darlings as much as we are our own." (Ibid., chap. iv.)

The remedy is life. Christ can do nothing effectual *for* us save so far as He is *in* us and we *in* Him.

2. There was also, in Smith's day, the orthodox Theologian who was apt, says he, to rest in his creed as a spider in its crevice and weave out an endless web of notions.

"We have many grave and reverend idolaters that worship truth only in the image of their own wits; that could never adore it so much as they may seem to do, were it anything else but such a form of belief as their own wandering speculations had at last met together in; were it not that they find their own image and superscription upon it." (" The True Way . . . ," p. 2.)

But this is mere learned ignorance; mere formal contact with the body and outside of truth.

"Divine truth is better understood as it unfolds itself in the purity of men's hearts and lives than in all those subtile niceties into which curious wits may lay it forth. And, therefore, our Saviour, who is the great master of it, would not, while He was here on earth, draw it up into any system or body, nor would His disciples after Him; He would not lay it out to us in any canons or articles of belief, not being indeed so careful to stock and enrich the world with opinions and notions, as with true piety, and a God-like pattern of purity, as the best way to thrive in all spiritual understanding. His main scope was to promote a holy life, as the best and most compendious way to a right belief. He hangs all true acquaintance with divinity upon the doing God's will. 'If any will do His will, he shall know of the doctrine whether it be of God.' This is that alone which will make us, as Peter tells us, 'that we shall not be barren or unfruitful in the knowledge of our Lord and Saviour.'" ("The True Way . . .," p. 12.)

Perhaps we, too, may have special need of the lesson—though possibly for another reason. Our danger may arise not so much from barren orthodoxy, or speculative dogmatism, as from a state of unsettling doubt. We have claimed our freedom to think, but claimed it at a great and, as some of us may have found, a very painful cost. We welcomed the critic with a light heart. We handed over to him our sacred treasures—received from the lips of father and mother, preacher and teacher. Old creeds; old views of the world and human life; the Old Testament and the New—we said, take them all, put them all to the test. And we are as sure as ever that we could not honestly have done otherwise. We are as sure as ever that the right of the critic to be, and to be heard, is incontestable. We are as sure as ever that his method on the whole is a sound one: that his call for a frank unbiassed endeavour to discover the fact, in every case, is the one course which love of truth dictates. But what havoc he may have wrought; how few of our early treasures has he seemed to return unscathed; how even the best things, even God Himself and Christ and the soul and the whole spiritual world, have seemed at times to be dissolving away; how cold and dark has seemed the loneliness when we have felt, perhaps, that we could not even pray!

Doubt—a blank tumult of the mind—we may know it well, or we may have it yet to face; and the temptation arising from it may be twofold. On the one hand, we may be tempted to banish doubt by an act of intellectual violence. We may turn on "reason" and revile it as a deceiver. We may succumb to a despair of ever walking in the light; and may clasp the hand of any plausible guide who cries with an air of authority: "This is the way, walk ye in it." On the other hand, we may be tempted to make the critical understanding supreme; to think that it alone can solve the doubts which its free use has created; to conclude, when it fails to solve them, when, rather, it intensifies and widens them, that there is no escape from their distracting and benumbing sway. But there is a better way—at least so far as spiritual truth is concerned. Of such truth, the critical understanding can never do more than touch the form, the shell, the husk. Its essence abides; and waits to enter by a lowlier door. There *is* a faith—a faith in God, in Christ, in the soul, in the great realities of which these are the centre—there is a faith which comes of self-control: the self-control which binds us firmly to the primal duties, the simple virtues, the clear behests of conscience.

"When Zoroaster's scholars asked him what they should do to get winged souls, such as might soar aloft in the bright beams of Divine truth, he bade them bathe themselves in the waters of life: they asking what *they* were, he tells them, the four cardinal virtues which are the four rivers of Paradise."

> I search my heart—I search and find no faith.
> Hidden He may be in its many folds—
> I see Him not revealed in all the world.
> Duty's firm shape thins to a misty wraith.
> No good seems likely. To and fro I am hurled.
> I have no stay—only obedience holds—
> I haste, I rise, I do the thing he saith.
>
> GEORGE MACDONALD. *The Diary of an Old Soul.* Stanza, 9 February.

NOTE.—The Discourse on the "True Way of Divine Knowledge" affords a good example of Smith's manner of using the Platonists, etc. They are used to illustrate what he is already sure of. In this case assurance has its foundation in experience supported by Scripture— Ps. cxi. 10 and John vii. 17; and by some striking sentences in Clemence Alexander, strom. 3. These, there- fore, are put together on the first page. But flashes of light conveyed in striking phrases or sentences from the Stoics, from Socrates, from Pythagoras, from Plutarch, from Plato and Plotinus especially, are thrown off as often as he needs them. They are ready at hand— on the tip of his pen—the moment his memory calls for them. Plotinus, most of all, is found helpful. The result is like a piece of music where the dominant theme is enriched by the irruption of melodious notes, e.g. "God is best discerned νοερᾷ ἐπαφῇ, as Plotinus phraseth it, by an intellectual touch of him: we must 'see with our eyes and hear with our ears, and our hands must handle the word of life,' that I may express it in St. John's words."

"The soul itself hath its sense, as well as the body;

and therefore David, when he would teach us how to know what Divine goodness is, calls not for speculation but sensation. ' Taste and see how good the Lord is.' " " Divinity is not so well perceived by a subtle wit as by a purified sense—ὥσπερ αἰσθήσει καθαρμένῃ, as Plotinus phraseth it."

CHAPTER IV

RALPH CUDWORTH (1617–1688)

RALPH CUDWORTH, the most erudite of the Cambridge men, was born at Aller in Somerset, two and a half miles north-west of Langport—fifteen years before John Locke's birth at Wrington, twenty miles further north.

His father had been a Fellow of Emmanuel, and Aller was a college living given him when he ceased to be minister of St. Andrew's, Cambridge, perhaps on the occasion of his marriage. In 1624 his father died; and after a time, his mother married a Dr. Stoughton, by whom the boy was educated until he entered Emmanuel as a pensioner on 9 May, 1632. It is said that, as a result of his not having had a public-school training, he was less expert than some of his rivals; but his election to a Fellowship in 1639, and his uncommon success as a tutor, are a fair proof of scholarly distinction. In 1645 he became master of Clare Hall, and (15 October) Regius Professor of Hebrew. He owed these appointments to the Parliamentary Commissioners acting with the Earl of Manchester; and they imply that he was regarded as a Puritan. But his Puritanism, like that of Whichcote, was far more a matter of ethical temper, or even political sympathy, than theological agreement. Certainly he did not hold the Calvinistic creed. In 1668 he wrote to his friend Limborch of Amsterdam—head of the Remonstrant, or Arminian, party—a letter,[1] in which he told how he had imbibed the doctrines of Calvinism almost with his mother's milk, and had been imbued with them (by Dr. Stoughton?) as a youth; how, nevertheless, the force of truth broke through all early prejudices when he came to Cambridge. What began his emancipation was a study (in which he delighted) of the ancient Philosophers, not only the Peripatetic sort, but also the Platonic; but what made it complete was his consideration of ethical principles. For the more he considered these, the more clearly he saw that *boni et mali moralis naturas esse prorsus immutabiles, nec revera ab ipsius Dei arbitrio pendere.* Hence, he soon found it impossible to hold by "*horrenda ista decreta,*" by which God out of his mere pleasure (*ex mere beneplacite*) damned men to eternal torments without fault or conscious sin of their own. It seemed to him absolutely clear that the assertion of such a decree did away with the very nature of sin. Accordingly, when he disputed for his doctor's degree in 1653, the thesis he undertook to defend was this: *boni et mali rationes eternas et immutabiles.*[2] He says that some of the doctors who opposed him told him afterwards in private that they did so "*pro more*" rather than from conviction, because they feared lest the acceptance of *this* thesis should overturn their beloved Calvinism from the foundation (*quasi Veritas posset Veritatem labefactare*). From that time, however, very many in the

[1] The Latin original is quoted by Von Hertling in his *John Locke und die Schule von Cambridge* (1892), p. 164.

[2] Tulloch and others, therefore, are mistaken in quoting this thesis as directed first against Hobbes.—Hertling, ibid., p. 164, n.

University—persuaded (he thinks) by the truth's own evidence—went over to the camp of the Remonstrants. This is valuable testimony to the state of Cambridge in 1653 and later, when, to all appearance, the Calvinists had regained the upper hand; and with it agrees what his daughter (afterwards Lady Masham) wrote to Limborch (September 1695), viz.—"these doctrines" (Calvinistic) "had come to be little thought of before I came into the world [1]; and Mr. Locke used to speak of the opinions" (Remonstrant) "that I had always been accustomed to at Cambridge, even among the clergy there, as something new and strange to him." [2] Locke belonged to Oxford where, during his time (1652–1658), the ruling spirits, whether Presbyterian or Independent, were mostly Calvinist. It was from Cambridge that the influence came which set him free from the narrowness of his early training.[3] That Cudworth made no secret of his Arminian tenets is demonstrated by the sermon preached before the House of Commons (31 March, 1647), from which I have quoted above.[4] It breathes the spirit of Whichcote from end to end. He was but thirty, and had his future at stake. Yet just then, when "the tension of Party-spirit was at its height, and every question, theological and national, which divided the factions, assumed an exaggerated bulk in the imaginations of men and intensified their antipathies"; just then, with Cromwell present, and an audience of Presbyterian M.P.s resentful of the Inde-

---

[1] She was born in 1658.

[2] Fox Bourne's *Life of Locke*, vol. ii. 282. In May 1691, Limborch wrote to Locke: "Among all my English friends the one I always most esteemed was Dr. Cudworth."

[3] Ibid., vol. i. 77, 310.   [4] Ante, p. 43.

pendent ascendency which he stood for, Cudworth
lifted up his voice like a trumpet; called them off from
their party differences as from mere trifles; and called
them to the life of Christ as the pith and kernel of all
religion. He evinced the fearless courage of a prophet,
for once at least; and this inclines one to believe that if,
on any future occasion, he seemed to play the flatterer,
it was in appearance only.

On 3 October, 1650, he succeeded Whichcote in the
Rectory of North Cadbury. Whichcote came back to
be the Head of King's College; and Cudworth would
fain have stayed on at Clare Hall but for the fact that
he was suffering "through want of maintenance." This
sounds unlikely, till we learn that he had "a difficulty
in obtaining the stipend of his Mastership." However,
his exile was not for long. In October 1654 he attained
a position which set him above care. He was elected
Master of Christ's College—the college of Milton and
Henry More, the latter of whom is said to have declined
the post. He was now able to marry and settle down.
Here were born to him a son, Thomas, and a daughter,
Damaris. Here, with rare visits to London, he lived
in and for his work. Here he died (26 June, 1688) and
was buried in the college chapel.[1] Now and then he had
contact with the outside world of affairs—perhaps more
often than is recorded. We hear of him as one of the
committee convened by Cromwell to advise him about
the admission of the Jews to England (1655), and it
is plain from some of his extant letters that statesmen
like Whitelocke and Thurlow consulted him—the former,

[1] His widow went to reside with her daughter Lady Masham
at Oates, and lived till 1695.

e.g. "about a proposed revision of the English version (King James's) of the Scriptures"; and the latter "about suitable and trustworthy men qualified for civil appointments under the Government." But Christ Church was his world. Its claims upon him were his first concern; and his books came next. He had no time to spare for his Vicarage of Ashwell in Hertfordshire, presented to him (in 1662) by Sheldon, Bishop of London; nor, perhaps, for the duties of his Prebend (1678) at Gloucester. He felt himself dedicated to literary tasks which might well excuse him for neglect of ordinary clerical work.[1] But these tasks were too big, or planned on too big a scale. While every day added to the mass of his learning, his power to use it for the work he had in hand seems to have grown less and less. He was hampered and hindered by his tools. Hence the fact that, after the sermon of March 1647, he published little or nothing before 1678. Henry More, in the Preface to his *Grand Mystery of Godliness* (1660), goes into raptures over a dissertation of Cudworth's on the Seventy weeks in the Book of Daniel, declaring it to be "of as much price and worth in theology as either the circulation of the blood in physic or the motion of the earth in natural philosophy." But for some reason he did not publish it; and it now lies among a heap of his other papers in the British Museum. Again, we read in the letter to Limborch already quoted that he had long been intending to follow up his first dissertation on the nature of good and evil with a whole system of ethics which should circle round the theme "*de bono et malo Justo*

---

[1] He was one of an increasing number of clergy who did likewise without any prick of conscience.

et injusto φύσει "; but he had done little more than
meditate, whereas his friend and colleague, More—with
no thought of snatching an advantage—had both
meditated and accomplished a book on the same subject. Cudworth made a grievance of this, and an excuse
for desisting from his purpose, "lest it should seem as
if we were fighting for our own glory." So it was not
till 1678—the year of "Habeas Corpus" and the first
edition of *Pilgrim's Progress*—that he justified to the
world that immense reputation for unique proficiency
"in all the choicest kinds of philosophy" which he
enjoyed among his friends.[1] For there is no doubt that
The True Intellectual System of the Universe, published
in that year, is, with all its defects, one of the most
amazing monuments of "promiscuous learning" ever
written. Yet it was but a fragment of what he intended
—"the propylæum, or at least first inner court of a
vaster structure that was to have its penetralia behind."
It turned out, however, to be all there was to be. The
builder did not attempt to finish the temple thus
grandly begun. What held his hand seems to have been
disgust, or weariness, or both. He found himself without
the necessary encouragement, or mental energy. For
his work fell almost still-born from the press. The few
who pretended to read it, turned away contemptuous
or hostile, and spread a report of it which disturbed a
whole nest of hornets. Some said he had raised stronger
objections against the Being and Providence of God

[1] See More's Dedication of his *Conjectura Cabbalistica* (1653)
to Cudworth. His acquisitions in any subject (says More) were
"enough to fill if not to swell an ordinary man with great conceit
or pride." More adds "that there was no conceit or pride in
Cudworth. He is no more imperious or censorious of others
than they ought to be that know the least."

than he could answer, and that he was a Tritheist or an Arian or a Socinian or a Deist; some that, under pretence of defending Revelation, he had written against it in the way of "an artful infidel"—and so on. "Thus ran the popular clamour. Would the reader know the consequence? Why the zealots inflamed the bigots. 'Twas the time's plague, when madmen led the blind. The silly calumny was believed; the much injured author grew disgusted; his ardour slackened; and the rest, and far greatest part of the defence, never appeared." But the truth is that by 1678, Cudworth had drifted into a new world. The strenuous and serious thoughtfulness of his earlier days had mostly passed away. People had no taste for the great questions which absorbed his interest; still less for his massive treatment of them. They were bent on frivolities, or a brisk handling of moral and religious things which should be level to the meanest understanding. Amid such an environment, a scornful indifference to his work, or a shallow criticism of it, was assured. Nor could the wider and truer appreciation of its merits which came later,[1] save it from being anything more than a rich quarry to which an occasional student has been indebted for apt quotations and curious references.

Martineau has condensed Cudworth's Philosophy,[2] which he describes as essentially a theory of knowledge; and has pointed out the organic connection between

[1] Thomas Wise published an abridgment in two volumes (1706). Le Clerc in 1703 began analyses of its arguments, etc., which continue through nine volumes of his *Bibliothèque Choisie*. In 1733 Mosheim published in Leyden a Latin translation with valuable notes, etc. This was rendered into English in 1845 by John Harrison.

[2] *Types of Ethical Theory*, vol. ii. 406 ff. (Library Edition).

this and his ethical doctrine. The latter is a deduction, to Cudworth himself a necessary deduction, from the former. But it is not too much to say that he valued his metaphysics chiefly on account of the ethics which it sustained. Two or three sentences of Martineau's will make this clear.

"The 'Intelligible Ideas' . . . are eternal and necessary modes of the Divine Mind; and from that infinite seat they pass into the finite world in two distinct, yet related, ways; by an act of God's Will, things are called into existence of which they become the essences: by a lending of *His Spirit* to centres of dependent being, and communication of *His Consciousness*, they become the intuitive lights of Reason and Conscience for all free natures: and thus, they guide us, on one line, to the true reading of the universe, and on the other, to the immediate sympathy of God. Hence it is that all men have the same fundamental ideas, to form the common ground both of intellectual communion and of moral co-operation." [1]

Mind in God and mind in man are the same. The rational, therefore, is the real—whether it appear under the aspect of intellectual or moral truth—is the real and immutable. Martineau's criticism of Cudworth's position in the light of modern psychology is perhaps unanswerable; but of its substantial soundness he is a wholehearted exponent.

In the "Intellectual system" Cudworth did not get as far as its application to ethical doctrine. But his mind was so full of the moral issue that, although he dropped his pen as regards the rest of his system, he took it up

[1] *Types of Ethical Theory*, vol. ii. 414 ff. (Library Edition).

again to write a *Treatise on Immutable Morality*, which was found (incomplete and unrevised) after his death, and published in 1731 by Dr. Edward Chandler (1668?– 1750), Bishop of Durham. We have no choice, therefore, but to take this insistence on the moral issue as his characteristic feature. All the Cambridge men, as we have seen, put morals first. They are first in respect of Religion, and equally first in respect of Philosophy. But Cudworth gives them the first place with special emphasis. That the truths of Philosophy and Religion are a guiding and kindling light for the conduct of life—was virtually his motto, as it was also Plato's. "The soul of Plato's philosophy" — to quote Professor Blackie — "lies in morals, as everyone must feel who will breathe, some time, with serious sympathy the atmosphere of his works. In this respect, there is nothing more striking than to compare the serious moral tone that winds up his dialogues, with the chain of moral maxims, with which St. Paul generally concludes his doctrinal epistles. After eleven chapters of somewhat perplexed and puzzled argumentation—the great Apostle—to take one example from many—proceeds, in the twelfth chapter of the Epistle to the Romans, to discharge a whole battery of the most important practical admonitions, as if eager to make it manifest to his readers that all argumentative theology is a necessary evil, which one must accept only as a traveller does a long dark tunnel, through which it is necessary that he should pass before he can emerge into the freedom of a broad and smiling landscape." The Professor would have come nearer the truth if he had spoken of a long brightening passage breaking its way, with a promise of escape, to entombed miners.

But he was right in what he meant, that St. Paul had in view a moral Salvation as the end and aim of his Gospel; and that Plato had the same thing in view as the end of his dialectic. The *Gorgias*, which Blackie cites in proof, is an apt illustration. Beginning with a dialectical dissection of the idea of eloquence, it works out the argument to a moral note of deep solemnity— "Of all that has been said nothing remains unshaken but the saying that to do injustice is more to be avoided than to suffer injustice, and that the reality and not the appearance of virtue is to be followed above all things as well in public as in private life, and that when anyone has been wrong in anything, he is to be chastised, and that the next best thing to a man being just is that he should become just; also, that he should avoid all flattery of himself as well as of others, of the few or of the many: and Rhetoric and any other art should be used by him, and all his actions should be done always, with a view to justice."[1] One is reminded of what has been observed, to the like effect, about Kant:

"The greatest business of man is to know what man must be in order to be man." All else is preliminary to ethics. "The problem of conduct was for him the supreme problem of philosophy."

As to Cudworth, the bearing of Philosophy on morals was brought home to him in a very urgent way by the baleful influence of Hobbes (1588–1679). Another influence—that of Descartes—conspired with Hobbes', inasmuch as the Frenchman also taught a doctrine of God which abolished "the just and good φύσει." "The will of God," he said, "creates all moral distinc-

[1] Jowett's translation.

I

tions, and, by arbitrary choice, turns into good and bad things that would else be indifferent, so that by a reversed volition of his, virtue and vice would change places. Thus far the Divine absolutism had been carried by many theologians"; but Descartes "pushed it further to its logical terminus, and maintained that nothing was true or false except by the will of God, so that it was at his option to make the three angles of a triangle equal to two right angles or to any other number."[1]

Cudworth does not overlook Descartes; but Hobbes was the man whom he dreaded—because of his vogue with the man in the street. Few men have so deeply stirred the minds of his fellows as the author of the *Leviathan.* "Hardly has there been seen again such a ferment of popular feeling and learned opinion round the thought of one man till, in these days, Darwinism touched the same human interest in a manner not wholly dissimilar." The Philosopher of Malmesbury, wrote Warburton in 1741, "was the terror of the last age as Tindal and Collins have been of this. The press sweat with the controversy; and every young churchman militant would needs try his arms in thundering upon Hobbes' steel-cap." Of course the reason is plain, and was enough to justify the uproar, if anything could be.

One might fairly say that what he did was to take "Motion" from Descartes and make it, together with matter in the form of Atoms, the key to all that man knows, is, and does. Motions in the outer world of space set up motions in the several organs of sense, which, being passed on to the brain again, set up the motions which are called sensation, perception, imagination,

[1] Martineau, ut supra, p. 416.

memory, desire, will. Perhaps that may seem not far
wrong, even judged by the latest Physiology. But the
Physiology and Psychology of Hobbes were one and
the same. Motion not merely evokes but creates and
constitutes mental faculty. He held that man's sensa-
tions, imaginations, thoughts, emotions are all mere
"appearances" of motions in the interior parts of
his body.

Yet Hobbes in his own opinion was an orthodox
Christian and churchman. He disliked the Puritans and
their extempore prayers, but attended regularly the
services of the Episcopal Church, and always defended
her doctrines. No man, too, knew the letter of Scripture
better than he, or could quote it more aptly for his
purpose. The *Leviathan* in many of its chapters is a
perfect mosaic of Scriptural quotations, "The very title
itself, and the titles of its several books are Biblical."
He was quite as anxious to sustain all he advanced by
the authority of Holy Scripture as by general reasonings.
Nor was this simply a mask. He was not consciously
insincere or dishonest. But he took his Divinity entirely
on trust. It had nothing to do with Philosophy. "The
subject of Philosophy," said he, "is every body of whose
generation or properties we can have any knowledge."
"Therefore it excludes Theology or the doctrine of
God . . . it excludes the doctrine of angels and all such
things as are thought to be neither bodies nor properties
of bodies. It excludes history as well natural as political.
. . . It excludes Astrology and Magic. . . . It excludes
such knowledge as is acquired by Divine inspiration or
revelation, as not derived to us by reason but by Divine
Grace, in an instant and as it were by some sense super-

natural. It excludes the doctrine of God's worship as being not to be known by natural reason, but by the authority of the Church, and as being the subject of faith and not of knowledge." Thus Philosophy might go on to conclusions utterly irreconcilable by reason to the dogmas of the faith. But that did not matter. These were safe. He revered them. He swallowed them wholesale. And, meanwhile, it was a tribute to his reverence for them if he decked his Philosophy with sentences from the Oracle which set them forth. Could there be a more impressive warning of what may happen when Philosophy and Faith are made to stand apart?

Whichcote and Smith do not mention Hobbes; and, strange to say, More, the most spiritual of the group, is comparatively mild in his references to him. He does, indeed, feel, in conducting his argument as to the nature and immortality of the soul, that Hobbes is a formidable opponent; and does his best to overturn some of his positions. But even in doing so, he speaks of him with a certain respect. He is "our most confident and potent adversary" and is endowed with "an extraordinary quick-sightedness in discerning the best and most warrantable wayes of salving all Phenomena from the ordinary allowed properties of matter." [1] Perhaps, as Tulloch thinks, "the very distance and elevation of More's mind from the peculiar principles that animated Hobbes led him to look with comparative composure on the philosophy of the latter." Perhaps, too, the flattering remark may have reached his ears which Hobbes is said to have made—surely

[1] *The Immortality of the Soul* . . ., p. iii (1659). The first four chapters of this treatise are mostly concerned with Hobbes' materialism.

in an absent state of mind, or in a mood of irony, or out of ignorance—that if ever he found his own opinions untenable "he would embrace the philosophy of Dr. More." Anyhow, More seems never to have realised the bottomless gulf which divided Hobbes' system of thought from his own. Cudworth, however, was under no such delusion. He read the real significance of Hobbes from the first. He saw that Hobbes was directing a death-blow at the heart of sound religion and morality, in the name of Philosophy; and so he determined to put forth all his strength to counteract him. How he toiled to that end is visible in *The Intellectual System*— though Hobbes is not mentioned [1];—and it is pathetic to reflect how little came of his labour. If he did not exactly beat the bush without starting the hare, he beat up the dust as well to such an extent that the hare, when started, could hardly be seen. Nevertheless, if the reader has skill to omit and select he will find that the case against Materialism has seldom been put more cogently. His arguments are not new. They are as old as Plato and as modern as Martineau. For, as Berkeley said, "Philosophy has ever oscillated between those who place body first in the order of beings and make the faculty of thinking depend thereupon, supposing that the principles of all things are corporal; and others who —making all corporal things to be dependent on Soul

---

[1] In Mosheim's edition of *The Intellectual System* the index gives many references to Hobbes, but they are all to the Editor's notes, which are expository of indirect allusions in the text. For Cudworth, Hobbes is "a modern philosopher," or a "modern writer," or "a modern atheistical pretender" to wit, etc. Attention may be drawn to Mosheim's comprehensive note (vol. iii. pp. 502–7) on what he calls "the whole of Hobbes' Discipline" and Cudworth's Criticism.

or Mind—think this to exist in the first and primary sense, and the being of Bodies to be altogether derived from and presuppose that of the mind." It sounds like Hobbes speaking when Tyndall says, "Matter I define as that mysterious thing by which all this has been accomplished," i.e. the whole series of phenomena from the primal mist to the self-conscious life of man. On the other hand, when Martineau pleads that "man's mind—conscious of self and a not-self—is the highest term in nature; that it yields immediate certainty of its own spirituality; that if, in any sense, it had been evolved out of primordial atoms, it must first have been put into them, and so postulates a mind behind and above them"—it is only the language that is new; Cudworth said just the same. He asked Hobbes how, if "mind is nothing else but local motion in the organic parts of man's body," mind could ever have become self-conscious, and, at the same time, sure that it is more than mere motion; he asks whether motion, though you recede with it as far back as the original whirl of atoms, does not necessarily imply a first mover; he asks, is there not "a scale or ladder of nature and degrees of perfection and entity one above another . . . and if the sun be nothing but a mass of fire or inanimate subtle matter agitated, then hath the most contemptible animal that can see the sun and hath consciousness and self-enjoyment, a higher degree of entity and perfection in it than that whole fiery globe. . . . Cogitation is, in our own nature, before local motion. Wherefore, there being plainly a scale or ladder of entity, the order of things was unquestionably in way of descent from higher perfection downward to lower; it being as impossible for a greater perfection to be produced from a lesser, as for something to be caused by nothing."

"Mind is the oldest of all things, senior to the elements and the whole corporeal world"; and, likewise, it is "κατα φύσιν," "by nature lord over all" . . . and, though modern writers take little or no notice of this, yet did Plato anciently make it his chief business to maintain that "life and understanding, soul and mind are not juniors to body," but that on the contrary, it is the very notion of soul that it is "something self-moving and self-active, the cause of motion, not its effect, and, therefore, that body is the junior to soul both in man and in the Universe." Cudworth felt all the more confidence in his weapons that Plato had forged and wielded them long ago.

It was from Plato, too, that he drew the mainstay of the ethical doctrine which he opposed to that of Hobbes. The ethics of the latter was consistent with his psychology. If the soul itself was a compound of motion, its principles of right and wrong could not well be immutable. If it was the creature of sensible experience, *they* could hardly be spiritual, either in origin or character. If *it* came into being through the senses, all it contained, including right and wrong, must have come the same way. Conscience—whether conceived as an inner organ for the Divine voice, or a beam of the Divine light—could have no real existence. Accordingly, there is (said Hobbes) nothing "just and good φύσει" —i.e. by nature, whatever becomes just and good does so θέσει—i.e. by institution. His position is quite clear, and so are its consequences. Men's natural state (he says) is utterly selfish. Their strongest motion, or impulse, is towards bodily pleasure, because that helps vital action; and away from pain, because pain hinders it. Each has an equal right to all, if he can get it; and the more virtuous are they who show themselves the stronger. "Might is right." The immediate result, however, is universal misery; and the last result, did nothing intervene, would be mutual extermination. But Reason —i.e. a sense of what is required for self-preservation— persuades men to waive their common rights and accept the rule of a common outward authority. This authority, clothed with delegated power to make and enforce laws, is henceforth supreme. It becomes the fount—the sole fount—of law and order and retributive justice. Virtue consists in obeying it; sin is committed when a man "does or omits, says or wills anything contrary to the laws"; the moral sanction is simply fear of punishment and hope of reward. When God is brought on the scene, He is no more than the strongest of beings, who is supposed, somehow—by visible sign or audible voice—to have declared, under tremendous pains and penalties, certain things to be His will. But here, also, the civil government is supreme—it, above all, having the right to say, or interpret, what God has commanded, so that loyalty comprehends all morality, and the sin of sins is rebellion.

Of course, a bare sketch like this does not do Hobbes full justice: to do him full justice it is necessary to read him, and especially to remember the circumstances of his times, and his ardent desire to see the turmoils of war subdued within the bounds of a strong and lasting peace. But such a sketch is true so far as it goes; and is enough, at any rate, to indicate those features in

Hobbes' ethical doctrine which excited so deeply the repulsion—even the terror—of Cudworth. Basing himself on Plato, his first position is that there is a Divine mind, the eternal home of Truth, the ultimate seat of the εἴδη, the "Intelligible Ideas." These have never been created. God did not make them, nor can He unmake or even change them. They are as eternal and necessary as Himself. Of these ideas, especially those specifically moral, reason has intuitive and certain perception. They are common to God and man; they are the truths or principles which neither rise nor set, but shine always with the same constant and benignant light. To quote Cudworth's own words: "Good and evil, just and unjust, honest and dishonest (if they be not mere names without any signification) cannot possibly be arbitrary things, made by will without nature. . . ." Just as "Omnipotence itself cannot by mere will make a body triangular without having the properties of a triangle in it . . . or things . . . like or equal one to another without the nature of likeness and equality . . . so neither can God make the morally good and evil, just and unjust, honest and dishonest by mere will without any nature of goodness, justice and honesty." Such distinctions are absolute and unwavering; binding alike on God and man. There cannot, e.g. be two principles of justice—one for God and one for man. The nature of Justice is immutable. God's justice is simply the reality of that which is man's ideal. No doubt there are things called θέσει, things good or evil positively or institutionally—but even these gain all their force from some connection with things which are good or evil absolutely. Thus, if the laws put forth by a governor *ought* to be obeyed, it is either because they are seen intuitively to be right, or else it is because they are put forth by one whom we have promised to obey. Here then, obligation is rooted not in the mere will of the governor but in a natural law of truth. To disobey would be to break a promise. But even so the implied promise, and, therefore, the implied obligation, only extend to things indifferent. Accordingly, if something is commanded which is seen to be intrinsically wrong, the human is at once superseded by a Divine claim, and the obligation ceases. Nay—even with respect to laws Divine, if any of them are "positive," the scope and intent of them must be to subserve those which are absolute. As John Smith says—speaking of the old Jewish laws—God gave them for nothing else but this: to secure the eternal law of righteousness from transgression. Their purpose "was not merely to manifest His absolute dominion and sovereignty, as some think, but for the good of those that were enjoined to obey." From this standpoint, it was but a step to maintain, as the Cambridge men did, that the contents of any alleged Revelation, including the Christian, must not expect to be received and approved, if they, or so far as they, contradict the moral reason or conscience. They may transcend the present reach of reason, and yet it may be reasonable to believe them, if the concurring evidence for their Divine origin is sufficiently clear; but to believe them or profess to believe them, if they are intrinsically absurd or immoral, is to outrage the very constitution of the soul and to shake the pillars of the universe.

Thus Cudworth argued, and with an intensity of

conviction which arose from his clear apprehension of the tremendous consequences involved, for faith and life. We are now to take note of one reputed adherent of the new school who, on this vital issue, unwittingly betrayed it, and proved thereby how impossible it is to preserve the new wine in old bottles.

CHAPTER V

Arrested Development

NEITHER the birth of Culverwel nor his death can be exactly dated, nor can we be quite sure about his parentage. It has been assumed as certain [1] or probable [2] that he was a son of Ezekiel Culverwel (d. 1631), Incumbent successively of Great Stanbridge and Felsted (Essex), in which case he would have been distantly related to Dr. Laurence Chaderton (1536?–1640), the first Master of Emmanuel, and to Dr. William Whitaker (1548–1595), the distinguished Master of St. John's College, each of whom married a sister of Ezekiel, whose father Nicolas was a wealthy London merchant. Such a connection would go far to explain Nathaniel's "hearty Puritanism." But it seems much more likely that his father was Richard Culverwel, Rector (from 1618 to 1644) of St. Margaret's, Friday Street, London [3]: for the entry of his baptism occurs in the church register under date 13 January, 1618–19. [4] This would account for his being described, at matriculation, as "of Middlesex"; and it would put the date of his birth about December 1618.

[1] By Mullinger, iii. 630.   [2] By Tulloch, ii. 413.
[3] Where he was buried on 12 April, 1644.
[4] Venn, *Alumni Cantabrigienses* (1922).

130

Anyhow, "he was entered as a pensioner at Emmanuel 5 April,[1] 1633—became B.A. in 1636, M.A. in 1640; was elected a Fellow in 1642; and died not later than 1651." "He was, therefore, in the very centre of the Platonic movement in its earlier form. He must have heard Whichcote often preach . . . John Smith and he could hardly fail being friends—with so much in common."[2] He had a brother, Richard, Incumbent of Grindisburg, Suffolk, who wrote of him—from "my study" on 18 August, 1652—that Nathaniel's latter days were darkened by a strange mental trouble which affected his deportment so that, to strangers, he seemed "as one whose eyes were lofty and his eyelids lifted up, who bore himself too high upon a conceit of his parts." But those who knew him well, treated him with affectionate tenderness. Remembering his "noble and gallant abilities," they did but deplore the "sad discipline of Providence" which, for the moment, impaired their brightness. He died surrounded by the comforting influence of their sympathy. Of what he left behind, to illustrate his worth, eight sermons, entitled *Spiritual Opticks* (I Cor. xiii. 12), were issued by his friend William Dillingham (also a Fellow of Emmanuel) a few months after his death. "It was sent forth," he says, "like Noah's dove to make a discovery." Its good report encouraged the writer to "give wing to all its fellows." This was in 1652. Three other editions of the complete works followed—the second in 1654, the third in 1661, the fourth in 1669. Then oblivion overtook them for nearly 200 years. But in 1857 *The Discourse*

[1] So *D. N. B.*; but Venn gives the date as "April 16th." Both Richard and Ezekiel had been at Emmanuel before him.
[2] Tulloch, ii. 413.

of the Light of Nature obtained a goodly resurrection
at the hands of Dr. John Brown of Edinburgh, who
prefaced it with what biographical details he could
gather up; translated the hundreds of Latin, Greek and
Hebrew quotations; and added many illuminating
notes—all in a truly admirable way. Further, he got
his friend Dr. John Cairns of Berwick, to introduce the
Discourse with a Critical Essay. Like Dillingham, Dr.
Brown sent it forth "to make a Discovery," and had
"the other remains of Culverwel" ready for publication
if his dove brought back a favourable sign. But it found
no sufficient place for its feet. In other words, there
was no sufficient public for the *Discourse*; and so none
for the rest.

Tulloch justly claims for the *Discourse* the very
highest value in point of genius, and wealth of thought
and style. "Not even John Smith's *Discourses* are more
instinct with a lofty ideality and all the glow and beauty
of a luminous yet impassioned imagination." "It is
almost a poem in its grandeur and harmony of conception
and the lyrical enthusiasm with which it chants the
praises of Reason." This is true; and it is true, also, as
Dillingham said, that its literary style is "cloth of gold"
and "weaved of sunbeams."

"I would turn thee," he says, "to the beginning of
the seventeenth chapter. Never was light so bespangled,
never did it triumph in greater bravery of expression."
But Tulloch falls into two mistakes—one positive and
of no great account, the other negative and much more
serious. With regard to the former, he goes wrong when
he quotes Culverwel as "ridiculing the prevalent delusion
of the Cambridge school," viz. that the Jews were "the

source of all moral and spiritual knowledge" in Pythagoras, Plato, etc., and as being himself superior to such a folly. "Nowhere does Culverwel show higher sense and penetration." As a matter of fact, however, Culverwel's ridicule was not meant for his fellows of the Cambridge School at all; but for those who would have it, that Pythagoras and Plato *borrowed common notions* from the Jews and their "written laws." Certainly Whichcote, Smith, Cudworth and even More never dreamed of saying this, because it was the pith and marrow of their contention that common notions and the moral law are discoverable by that "Light of nature," that "Candle of the Lord," which they, no less than Culverwel, believed to be the birthright of every man. What they did—or rather what Cudworth did in a small degree and More in a greater—was to suppose that some parts of Greek Philosophy, the Atomic theory, e.g. had been derived from a legendary Moschus or Mochus who was really Moses. So far as I am aware, this was all they did; and Culverwel did just the same. For he says it "must be granted that the whole generality of the heathen went agleaning in the Jewish fields. They had some of their grapes, some ears of corn that dropped from them." [1]

But it is a matter of greater concern to note the mistake of omission which underlies Tulloch's remark that "In the *Discourse* . . . little remains of his Puritan Calvinism, save its distilled and purer essence of spiritual rapture. A few traces of dogmatic narrowness are manifest here and there, but never in a harsh form . . ." (ii. 414).

---

[1] Tulloch quotes these words on the same page as the statements which may be said to cancel them (ii. 424).

It is evident from this that Tulloch omitted to give due weight to those "few traces of dogmatic narrowness" in the *Discourse*; and, still more, to read Culverwel's sermons. Hence he failed to see what needs to be made clear, viz. the persistence and triumph in Culverwel of that harsh element in Calvinism against which Whichcote and his friends protested.

1. Nothing said or written by Whichcote or Smith is in a higher strain of admiration for Reason than we find in the *Porch*, or introduction to the *Discourse*, and in later parts of it. Nor was he a whit less hard on the people who decry Reason. "To blaspheme reason is to reproach heaven itself, and to dishonour the God of Reason, to question the beauty of the image." "What would these railers have? Would they be banished from their own essence? Would they forfeit and renounce their understanding? Or have they any to forfeit or disclaim? Would they put out the candle of the Lord, intellectuals of His own lighting? Or have they any to put out? Would they creep into some lower species, and go agrazing with Nebuchadnezzar among the beasts of the field? Are they not there already? Oh! what hard thoughts those men have of religion! Do they look upon it only as a bird of prey, that comes to peck out the eyes of men?"

2. True, Reason is now "a diminishing light." The "fall" of man entailed the falling upon him of a "sudden cloud which blotted all his glory."

"Sin entered in first at a corporeal, then at an intellectual window, and stole away the heart, and the windows have been broken ever since."

This accounts for man's feeble understanding of

Spiritual things—of himself—of Angels—of God, although these "have most of entity and so most of intelligibility." It explains, also, "the black and prodigious errors" which have overtaken men, as if their candle were quite blown out.

Culverwel enumerates, as in point, "the blundering Antinomian," "The Vagabond Seeker," "the wild seraphic," or enthusiast—"set on fire of hell." What but the "miserable weakness" of "their understanding" could betray men into such "thick and palpable darkness"! True, their candle was bright enough to guide them better if they had carefully followed it. The candle itself—their own reason—tells them this. But, all the same, it must have been a "feeble diminutive light"— too feeble for their need. So it is generally. There is light in the candle; and the light is enough to walk by. Then, why do men not walk by it? Because "this faint and languishing candle-light does not always prevail upon the will, it doth not sufficiently warm and inflame the affections." There is some confusion here. What men need, it now appears, is not so much light as more moral force—something to "prevail upon the will." Yet Culverwel's point against the alleged heretics was that their *light* had failed. Perhaps, like many other controversialists, he means to insinuate that ignorance, or a weak understanding, is the sign of a bad heart.

3. Nevertheless, although a "diminutive," Reason is a "certain" light. There is no ground for scepticism as to its ability to reveal knowledge. "Lamplight" may not be a "glorious" light but, so far as it goes, it is not "deceitful."

Culverwel is disdainful of all philosophical sceptics.

K

Based on the senses and the understanding, he is sure
that the truth of things is attainable and attained.
These two instruments, indeed, are not perfect. Errors
creep into sense; and then understanding, even if it
corrects the errors of sense, may make some new errors
of its own. But when the knowledge, resulting from
their conjoint action, is certified by its clearness, it is
unimpeachable. What is intuitively clear is convincingly
true. In this respect he is at one with Descartes.[1]

Truth, consequently, is within a man's reach. It is
something he can see for himself and be assured of
independently of external authority. He is not bound
to Plato or Aristotle, or the Church, or the Councils of
the Church. What these, and the like, offer him may,
and must, be tried by his own inward light. "For this
very end God hath set up a distinct lamp in every soul
that men might make use of their own light. All the
works of men, they should smell of this lamp of the
Lord that is to illuminate them all. Men are not to
depend wholly upon the courtesy of any fellow-creature;
not upon the dictates of men; nay, not upon the votes
and determinations of angels: for if an angel from
heaven contradict first principles, though I will not say,
in the language of the Apostle, 'let him be accursed,'
yet this one may safely say, that all the sons of men are
bound to disbelieve him." (p. 206.)

"I shall always reverence a grey-headed truth, yet
if antiquity shall stand in competition with the lamp

---

[1] From whom, however, he differs, in that he would resolve
assurance not into "thinking that he thinks" but into "thinking
that he sees." "The certainty of sense is so great as that an oath—
that high expression of certainty—is usually, and may very
safely, be built upon it." (*Discourse* . . ., pp. 201, 203.)

of the Lord—though genuine antiquity would never do it—yet if it should, it must not think much if we prefer reason, a daughter of eternity, before antiquity, which is the offspring of time." (p. 212.)

"Let none, therefore, so superstitiously look back to former ages as to be angry with new opinions and displayings of light, either in reason or religion. Who dares oppose the goodness and wisdom of God? If he shall enamour the world with the beauty of some pearles and jewels, which in former times have been hid or trampled upon? If he shall discover some more light upon earth, as he hath let some new stars be found in the heavens?"

These quotations are meant to make it plain in what honour Culverwel professed to hold Reason. It is of divine origin, and nature and efficacy. It is a true light which lighteth every man coming into the world. It answers to the Logos of the fourth Gospel, and the "Christ within" of the Friends. It is diminished by sin, but cannot lead astray if faithfully obeyed. It comes from God, and leads to God, and, in its measure, reveals God.

One might say, therefore, that no higher degree of Revelation could ever do more than amplify and clarify its light; could never, at any rate, contradict it.

Such, surely, is one of Reason's own clearest deliverances.

But the strange thing in Culverwel is this—that when he approaches the sphere of what he calls faith he dismisses Reason. We might not think so, indeed, from statements like the following:

"One light," he says, "does not oppose another;

the light of faith and reason may shine together, though with far different brightness; the candle of the Lord is not impatient of a superior light; it would bear an equal or superior." (p. 220.) "A candle neither can nor will put out the sun; and an intellectual sun can, but will not, put out the lamp. The light of reason doth no more prejudice the light of faith, than the light of a candle doth extinguish the light of a star." (p. 221.) "Why should there be any . . . strife between faith and reason, seeing they are brethren? Do they not both spring from the same Father of Lights; and can the Fountain of Love and unity send forth any irreconcilable streams? Do you think that God did ever intend to divide a rational being, to tear and rend a soul in pieces, to scatter principles of discord in it? If God be pleased to open some other passage in the soul, and to give it another eye, doth that prejudice the former?" (p. 222.)

All this is excellent. It is the authentic voice of Whichcote, John Smith, Ralph Cudworth, Henry More. It prepares us to put the best construction on his further statement—which also might have been theirs:

"Revealed truths shine with their own beams; they do not borrow their primitive and original lustre from this 'candle of the Lord,' but from the purer light, wherewith God hath clothed and attired them as with a garment. God crowns His own revelations with His own beams. 'The Candle of the Lord' doth not discover them; it doth not oppose them; it cannot eclipse them. They are no sparks of reason's striking, but they are flaming darts of Heaven's shooting, that both open and enamour the soul. They are stars of Heaven's lighting; men behold them at a great distance twinkling in the dark. Whatsoever comes in God's name does either find or make a way." (p. 223.)

But presently we find that, in saying "Revealed truths shine with their own beams," he intends a different kind of light from the natural, a light which to Reason may be absolute darkness. Thus, by the light of his *candle* he can see that "some of the heathens pleased God better than others. Surely Socrates was more lovely in His eyes than Aristophanes; Augustus pleased Him better than Tiberius; Cicero was more acceptable to Him than Catiline, for there were more remainders of His image in the one than in the other—the one was of purer and nobler influence than the other." (p. 265.)

The same light would teach us that God has no favourites; but that "He who reverences him and lives a good life in any nation is welcomed by Him." But the supernatural light checks our charity and confuses our sense of justice. For he goes on—"The less wicked is, compared with the more wicked, good; the one shall have more mitigations of punishment than the other. Socrates shall taste a milder cup of wrath, whereas Aristophanes shall drink up the dregs of fury; if divine justice whip Cicero with rods, it will whip Catiline with scorpions. An easier and more gentle worm shall feed upon Augustus, a more fierce and cruel one shall prey upon Tiberius; if justice put Cato into a prison, it will put Cethegus into a dungeon." (p. 265.) Yet Culverwel is sure that the whole moral difference between these variously wicked men was due to the will of God. That Socrates turned out not so bad as Aristophanes, e.g. was simply because God gave to the one a measure of unconditional grace to improve his "naturals," which He denied to the other. Thus he says—"As take two several lutes. Let them be made both alike for essentials, for matter and form. If now the one be strung better than the other, the thanks is not due to the lute, but to the arbitrary pleasure of him that strung it. Let them both be made alike, and strung alike yet if the one be quickened with a more delicate and graceful touch, the prevailing excellency of the music is not to be ascribed to the nature of the lute, but to the skill and dexterity of him that did move it and prompted it into such elegant sounds." In other words, God's grace is arbitrary. God could have given, had He willed, as much grace to Aristophanes as to Socrates; and have given Socrates grace enough to save him altogether. Nay, had He so willed, He could have reversed the fate of the two without first effecting the least change in their actual moral state. So free is the Grace of God "that it might save the worst of the heathen and let go the rest; it might save an Aristophanes as well as a Socrates, nay, before a Socrates, as well as a Publican before a Pharisee." (p. 270.) Grace then can cancel moral distinctions: to use Culverwel's phrase, can "make them go out in a snuff."

Some five or six years after a *Discourse of the Light of Nature* he preached in the same place, Emmanuel College, a sermon entitled "The Act of Oblivion" (Isa. xliii. 25). It has many choice thoughts finely expressed; and some of them, taken alone, might suggest that his theology had grown broader or sweeter; that, in fact, he had said "good-night to John Calvin."

"There is not so much evil in sin as good in God. . . .

There is a vaster disproportion between sin and grace than between a spark and an ocean. Now who could doubt whether a spark could be quenched by an ocean? Thy thoughts of disobedience towards God have been within the compass of time; but His goodness hath been bubbling up towards thee from all eternity. He hath had sweet plots of free grace and gracious contrivances toward thee from all eternity." And how piercingly ethical is this—"Thou hast a book within thine own breast; and conscience hath the pen of a ready writer. It can write as fast as the soul can dictate. *Calumum in corde tingit*, and with an accurate pencil it can give thee a full portraiture of thy most closeted behaviour, of thy most reserved actions, of thy most retired motions; and though there be a curtain drawn over them here, yet they shall be made very apparent. God shall give conscience an imprimatur, and such works as thou wouldst have supprest shall be published to the eyes of men and angels, and the λόγος κριτικός shall pass censure upon them. Sins of the smallest print, of the most indiscernible character, shall be more clearly legible, and become as atomies in the presence of a sunbeam." But, in fact, the sermon was preached for the elect only; and emphasises the harshest features of Calvinism. Its theme is the grace of God and its specific object is to show how absolute it is. You may see this, he says, "if you look to the spring from whence it flows: that original goodness, that fountain—mercy in election . . . thou wert God's jewel from all eternity . . . He took thee as a jewel, out of the rubbish of mankind, out of the *massa corrupta*; and, in His due time, He means to polish thee and to set a glorious lustre upon thee. . . . God might have had great revenues of glory out of thy eternal ruin. . . . Two books were before Him. He might have writ thy name in His black book, with fatal and bloody characters; and made His justice glorious in thy misery and damnation. Aye, but He took the book of life, and, with the point of a Diamond, writ thy name *there*—thus to make His love wonderful in thy salvation." But, says the Preacher, you will still more admire the riches of His grace, if you look not only to its fountain (in election); but also to its "several" manifestations. "'Twas out of the riches of His grace," e.g. "that He planted thee in a place of light when He shut up and imprisoned the world in palpable darkness." 'Twas out of the riches of His grace "that salvation should wait upon thee so long. . . . Free grace follows thee, and pursues thee, and will not let thee go till thou hast a blessing. . . . Are there not many of the damned that must lie roaring there to all eternity that never tasted of so much goodness and long-suffering as thou hast done?

"Consider in what state thou wast all the while—an enemy, a Rebel, studying how to be damned; galloping to hell and destruction with full career, a scholar's pace. Who wast it now that stopped thee in thy course? . . .

"Consider the overpowering and efficacious work of grace. He must *force* thee to be happy and necessitate thee to salvation, and compel thee to come in. . . .

"Compare thyself with those that have had none of all this kindness shown unto them, such as God hath left to themselves in the severity of His justice, and this will be a goodly gloss upon free grace. . . . Thus, many

heathen have lived more accurately and exactly than
some Christians in their unregenerated condition, and
yet out of all ordinary possibility of salvation. Some
have desired more strength and, in their way, prayed
for it too . . . yet have gone without it. . . . He passed
by men of most admirable endowments, most rare
accomplishments that, in all probability, would have
done Him a great deal more honourable service than
thou hast done." Aristotle, for instance.

There is no uncertain sound here; and delivered as
it was just about the time when Whichcote's alleged
Arminianism was exciting alarm, and inspiring Tuckney's correspondence with him, the sermon sounds like
an orthodox flourish.

It comes to this, in Culverwel's view, that whatever
God wills must be right. The only question to decide
is, has He willed it? Now faith could not ask a better
proof than His own word, and the Bible is God's word:
"Those sacred and heavenly volumes" (he says) "that are
strung together as so many pearls, and make a bracelet
for the spouse to wear upon her hands continually."
Reason, therefore, must not interpose between anything
in the Bible and Faith. Whatever in the Bible is dark
to reason must be regarded by Faith as the higher
light. "For this is the voice of Nature itself, that whatever
God reveals must needs be true; and this common
principle is the bottom and foundation of all faith to
build upon." (p. 224.) "But God being truth itself—
eternal, inimitable truth; His word being the 'vehicle
of truth,' and all revelations, flowing from Him, shining
with the prints and signatures of certainty. His *naked
word* is a demonstration; and he that will not believe

a God is worse than a devil, he is the blackest infidel that was yet extant." (p. 225.)

Culverwel cites the case of Abraham. "Abraham's slaying of his son may seem a most horrid and unnatural act against the 'law written'[1] against 'the candle of the Lord,' yet being commanded and authorised by God Himself, the candle durst not oppose the Sun. That pattern of faith, the father of the faithful, does not dispute and make syllogisms against it; he does not plead that it is against common notions, that it is against demonstrations, for he had said false if he had said so; but he doth dutifully obey the God of nature, that high and supreme Law-giver, who by this call and voice of His did plainly and audibly proclaim, that for Abraham to kill his son, in these circumstances, was not against the law of nature. So that all the stress and difficulty will be to know whether God reveals such a thing or not. . . ." (pp. 225–6.) No doubt, but may we not say that as to things moral the stress and strain do not exist ? They are removed by the known character of God. To make clear that character, to educate the human conscience towards a fuller and deeper apprehension of God's essential goodness, truth and love, was the chief end of the process which reached its consummation in the Word made flesh, the image of God, the effulgence of His glory. Even the temptation of Abraham may be taken as marking a stage in that process—a means of teaching one whose moral ideals were largely determined by the ruling ideas of his age, that what God wanted: what alone could satisfy Him: was not the physical sacrifice of his son, but the spiritual sacrifice of himself.

[1] νόμος γραπτός.

And so, if you plead the word of God for something which does violence not merely to the primitive intuitions of natural conscience, but, still more, to the highest intuitions of a purified Christian conscience, you cancel the meaning and purpose of all revelation. Texts, many or few, may be in its favour; but it is not texts which can seal the Divinity of a fact or doctrine: it is its agreement with the clear truth of Christ—and of this truth the Reason, quickened and guided by the spirit of God, is the only possible judge. Hence it is that Calvinism as expounded by Culverwel, and much else adduced in the name of Scripture, have had to go. All appeals to faith on their behalf have been vain. For the faith demanded could only be blind—nay, could only be given at the cost of moral or intellectual suicide. If Reason, judging by the holiest light, compels you to pronounce this right or that wrong, this true or that false, you cannot but regard it as an ultimate authority, and no act of faith can be more sacred, or imperative, than trust in its discernment. This is not rationalism in the common sense of the term. In the common sense of the term rationalism seeks to preclude faith, or at least denies the duty or value of implicit faith—faith whose object has not yet been completely brought under the categories of the understanding. In the sphere of religion, therefore, it would make faith always dependent on a logical process; and would dictate refusal of what cannot be proved. But this is very different from the position just laid down. For the latter admits that religion, as a fact and power of life, begins usually with acts of faith. Men of humble and lowly heart do not reason first, and then believe. They believe, and live, and, perhaps, never consciously reason at all. Perhaps they never feel the need, or possess the power, to advance beyond the intuitive conviction that what they believe is the truth. Their knowledge may be analogous to "the intuition or instinctive perception of beauty in nature and art, which is independent of the logical or theoretical faculties, and which is often keenest and quickest in natures whose reasoning powers are feeble or untrained."

But what one would say is, that *such implicit acts of faith* are, at the same time, *implicit acts of the reason.* Unless they were, experience would not justify them. Because they *are*, they may be vindicated tc conscious thought. Just here, indeed, is where theology comes in. Theology is not religion; it is the explication of religion. "In religion as in all other spheres of human activity . . . there is present the underlying element of reason which is the distinctive characteristic of all the activities of a self-conscious intelligence; and the endeavour, by reflection, to elicit and give objective clearness to that element—to denote what our religious ideas mean, what conceptions of the object of worship and of our own spiritual nature are involved in them; on what grounds they rest and to what results they point; to trace their relations to each other and to other branches of knowledge; to infuse, in short, into the spontaneous and unsifted conceptions of religious experience, the objective clearness, necessity, and unity of thought— this is the aim of theological science." Consequently, if in the process of thought elements of faith come to light, which reason, in proportion to its enlightenment, finds contradictory of itself, these, *ipso facto*, are declared to be false, and not even an angel from heaven can warrant their reception. For one of the functions of conscious reason is to purify our intuitions from foreign or spurious admixtures; and reason, in this respect, is the mainspring of theological progress. Much may still remain to faith which reason has failed to overtake; vast tracts of mystery around a little circle of light. But the circle of light *is* light; and is one which reason is ever tending to enlarge. Mysteries, where God is the author of them, where they lie in the nature or circumstance of the object, are all so many truths waiting to be disclosed. And if you say—"Yes, waiting to be disclosed to faith," the remark is meaningless. Nothing can be disclosed or revealed *to* faith. You believe in the Trinity; and the Trinity, you say, is a great mystery; and you hope that some day it may be revealed. But, if ever it be revealed it will, so far, pass beyond faith, and take rank among things intelligible. Revelation, now and always, must have for end and result the clearing up of what before was dark to Reason. And we mean this, or ought to mean this, when we use another common phrase: when we say that "one day faith will be turned to sight." So far as sight relates to intellectual or spiritual objects it can never be other than rational. In this sense, faith may never be turned to sight completely. There may be always unexplored continents—ample room for faith. But, so far as the change from faith to sight goes on, what else can sight be than insight: An ever-growing power of comprehending and realising truths hidden, or not clearly grasped, before? And so Reason no less than faith belongs to that which abides.

As Culverwel himself puts it in the last sentence of his *Discourse*:

"This candle of the Lord may shine here below, it may and doth aspire and long for happiness; but yet it will not come near it, till He that lighted it up be pleased to lift it up to Himself, and there transform it into a star, that may drink in everlasting light and influence from its original and fountain light."

To sum up. We may say of Culverwel that fundamentally he agreed with Whichcote; but he was inconsistent, either because he fell behind his teacher in measuring the scope of their common principle, or, what is more likely, because he had less courage to follow it up. And so, one time, he is found extolling Reason to the skies and willing to test everything by its light; but, at another, when a theology which he dare not abandon seems to demand it, he reduces reason to the position of a reluctant slave who must say "yes" when he would fain say "no." The phenomenon is not an infrequent one, nor need it imply deliberate self-deception. But in a scholar of Whichcote it was absurd; and is proof that Culverwel cannot be fairly reckoned as one of the same band as Smith or Cudworth. Especially to the latter would such inconsistency appear intolerable—a practical denial of all real significance in the new movement. For if that movement had any practical purpose, it was—from the standpoint of first principles—to break down the antinomy then so commonly preached between the faith of Philosophy and the faith of Religion. It aimed to do this, in particular, on the ethical side. And that one who started with so high a conception of the inner light should come to assert that, in matters of fundamental morality, the "candle of the Lord" might actually be darkness, must have been to Cudworth, with a stern fight for immutable moral laws against Hobbes on his hands, nothing less than betrayal.

CHAPTER VI

HENRY MORE (1614–1687)

I𝐹 Cudworth was the most erudite of the Cambridge men, Henry More was the most spiritual and mystical—a soul compact of light and fire. He was born in 1614 at Grantham, Lincolnshire. His father, Alexander, "a gentleman of fair estate and fortune," was that somewhat rare phenomenon, a non-Puritan Calvinist. In other words, he held strictly by Calvinism, and yet, at the same time, by the Church and the king's cause. His devotion to the king's cause and the Church was partially shared by his son; but not his devotion to Calvinism.

In the winter nights Mr. More used to read aloud Spenser's Rhymes, especially that "incomparable piece of his, the *Faery Queen*"—a circumstance to which Henry ascribes the first development of his poetic taste. Yet More senior had no wish for his boy to cultivate poetry or even scholarship, if this meant leaving the open road to wealth.

But the boy chose his own course. At the age of fourteen he was sent to Eton. From Eton, after three years, he entered Christ's College, Cambridge (December 1631) —about seven months before Milton left it. He took his Bachelor's Degree in 1635, his Master's in 1639, and immediately afterwards was chosen Fellow of his College. "This was his first promotion, and it may almost be said to have been his last."

"Many offers of preferment were subsequently made to him,[1] but he persistently refused them all, with one exception. Fifteen years after the Restoration, or in 1675, he accepted a prebend in Gloucester Cathedral, only to resign it almost immediately in favour of Dr. Edward Fowler, afterwards the well-known Bishop of Gloucester. The suspicion was that More only accepted the office in order to pass it on to Fowler." He seems to have held the living of Ingoldsby, an advowson which he had inherited from his father; but at the end of one year he passed it on to his friend John Worthington. In fact, he had no love for any work beyond the gates of his College. He had no ambition, and steadily declined every attempt to draw him into a public position. He would not even accept the Mastership of his College. Other offers of the Provostship of Trinity College, Dublin, and the Deanery of St. Patrick's shared the same fate. He had set his heart on the quiet privacy of his life as a Fellow, and as such he lived and died.[2] The precincts of Christ's College remained his home, and here, it is said, he had made a sort of paradise for himself.

Noble friends importuned him; the royal favour even solicited him to accept some office more worthy of his reputation. "Pray be not so morose," one noble person is represented as saying, "or humoursome as to refuse all things you have not known so long as Christ's College."

[1] Deanery of Christ Church (£900 per annum), Provostship of Trinity College, Dublin, Deanery of St. Patrick's, Dublin, two bishoprics (one £1,500 per annum), says Ward, pp. 58–9.

[2] "I am reminded here of what the Venetians used to say of Father Paul's cell, when they showed it unto strangers, viz. this was the Paradise in which a good Angel dwelt." Ward, p. 60.

But he was not to be moved. His friends even got him "on a day, as far as Whitehall, in order to the kissing of the Royal hand"; but when he understood that the condition of his doing so was the acceptance of a bishopric, "he was not upon any account to be persuaded to it." [1] Nothing, in short, could separate him for long from his college paradise.

Many happy days he spent there—says his biographer —and so "sweet and pleasing was the fruit of his solitary labours and musings that they often appeared to him on looking back upon them as an aromatick field." Once his father came to see him, not at all pre-disposed to approve his manner of life. But "coming into the room he was most highly affected with it, and, in a rapture, said . . . that he thought he spent his time in an angelical way." Perhaps it was more the air of comfort and luxury than the books that enraptured the old man. But, though he loved to be surrounded with beautiful things, More was no sybarite. In food and drink and dress his habits were simple. He took care, however, that they should be adapted to his taste. When he found that fish on Fridays, and fasting in Lent, and the college small beer did not suit him, he promptly gave them up. "Everyone," he said, "must follow his own constitution and best experience in these matters." [2]

More seems to have had a remarkable physique. He was tall and thin, of a "serene and vivacious" aspect, rather pale than florid, and his hazel eye vivid as an

[1] Tulloch, vol. ii. p. 325.
[2] Quoted from the *Life of More* by "Richard Ward, A.M., Rector of Ingoldsby, in Lincolnshire, 1710." A new edition of this, with "notes and Introduction by M. F. Howard," was published in 1911 (London: Theosophical Publishing Society).

eagle's. According to his own account his body was possessed of strange properties.[1] Certain products of it "had naturally the flavour of violets." "His breast and body, especially when very young, would of themselves, in like manner, send forth flowery and aromatick odours from them, and such as he daily almost was sensible of when he came to put off his clothes and go to bed."

For many years he enjoyed perfect health. His bodily frame seemed built for a hundred years; and he held it in such perfect control that it readily obeyed all the movements of his mind, and he was able to have his thoughts "oftentimes as clear as he could almost desire, and to take them off or to fix them upon a subject in a manner as he pleased."

After this there is no need to say that More was a happy man. He was happy every day and all day long. Sometimes he felt almost mad with pleasure—especially under the influence of nature or music. Many passages in his writings illustrate his delight in nature, and scarcely less was his delight in music. He played the "theorbo" (a large double-necked lute with two sets of tuning pegs, etc.),[2] and there were times when the pleasure became so keen as to be almost a pain, and he had to stop; while, at other times, he "found himself, in an extraordinary manner, recreated and composed by the sweetness and solemness of that instrument."

But if one were to conclude that More was an effusive person, it would be a mistake. On the contrary, he is said to have been reserved in manner, not talkative at

[1] Like those of the famous Valentine Greatrakes. Ward, pp. 123–5.
[2] See article "Theorbo" in Grove's *Dictionary of Music*.

any time, unless with those of his friends who were of kindred mind; and always self-restrained even when most raised and exalted inwardly. He loved silence because he found it so eloquent, and never felt less solitary than when alone.

More received "Holy Orders" about the time (1639) he was made Fellow of his college, and he wrote sermons: but whether he ever preached is not clear. "He made no secret of his attachment to the Church of England, at a time when it was dangerous to avow such sentiments; and he did not hesitate to use the Church Liturgy both in public and private when it was a crime to do so."

This is the statement of Canon Overton in the *D.N.B.* More's own statement in his *Grand Mystery of Godliness* (1660)—Address to the Reader—is less definite, and agrees better with the moderate position which made it possible for him to subscribe the Covenant.[1] Here he declines to commit himself to any specific theory of Church government, but expresses a preference for Thorndike's *Platform* [2] as "very accommodate to the present state of things; and, being such a mixture of Episcopacy and Presbytery together as may justly, if they could be modest and ingenuous, satisfy the expectations of both parties."

He had many pupils and spared no pains, or time, for their benefit; but writing was his chief employment. He is, indeed, the most literary of the school. Whichcote

---

[1] That he did so seems certain; and also the "Engagement" (Mullinger, iii. 596). Note that Whichcote evaded the Covenant, but took the Engagement; Cudworth and Smith took both.

[2] Thorndike (1598–1672) maintained "that the Reformation, as a durable settlement, was practicable only on the basis of a return to the discipline and teaching of the primitive Catholic Church." See *An Epilogue to the Tragedy of the Church* (1659).

wrote nothing. Smith wrote nothing for the press. Cudworth wrote much, but was slow to publish.

More, on the contrary, from 1642 down to within a year or two of his death, nearly always had something in the press. He, also, won the ear of the public as they never did. Some of his books ran through several editions. After his death, abridgments and extracts from his works were numerous. Before his death, "his writings were so much in vogue that Mr. Chishull, an eminent bookseller, declared that for twenty years together after the return of the king *The Mystery of Godliness* and Dr. More's other works ruled all the booksellers in London." In 1708 his theological works in folio were published at the expense of a "private Reverend and very worthy person out of a just sense of Honour to the Doctor, and, what is much more, the singular usefulness of his writings in this improved and improving age"—with confident expectation of a warm and wide reception; while a fourth edition of his Philosophical writings, "corrected and much enlarged," appeared in 1712. But there was another side. "'Tis very certain," wrote his biographer (Ward) in 1710, "that his writings are not generally (I will not say read but) as much as known, and many scholars themselves are in a great measure strangers to them." This came true soon, if it was not quite true then; and it has now long been true (as Tulloch says) that More "is the most interesting and the most unreadable of the whole band."

(1) He introduced himself in 1642 as a poet with what he called "Psychozoia Platonica—or, a Platonical Song of the Soul, consisting of four several Poems." This, with other similar effusions, was published in 1647 under the title *Philosophical Poems*. They are

biographically of interest for the dedicatory epistle to his father, to whose "encomiums of learning and Philosophy" he ascribes the impressions which first fired his "sedulous youth with the desire of the knowledge of things," however the father's "after advertisements" might seek to turn him off it. He also takes occasion to defend his father against some slanderous charge brought forward by a kinsman. He pays warm tribute to his "faithfulness," his "uprightness," his "sedulity for the public welfare" of Grantham, his generous openness and veracity.

But in relation to the author himself the interest of the book lies in the evidence it affords of his immersion, at that time, in Platonic "lore." "Plato" and deep "Plotin" are his confessed Masters. Through them he has found the key to "learned Pythagore Egyptian Trismegist, and the Antique rôle of Chaldee wisdom." He thinks some will "brand him with infamy" for his devotion; but he is defiant of their blame. They are the sort of people who brand Galileo and persist in refusing the truth of the new Astronomy "simply because it is at variance with the impressions derived from the sense." The blame of such people is praise.

(2) This was More's first stage—that of a young knight-errant in the service of truth—and his second stage prolonged to a large extent the inspiration of the first. In 1648 (December 7), he wrote the first of his four letters to Descartes, and eulogised him as the intellectual giant of his age, and welcomed the new Philosophy as the "most sober and faithful" that could be "offered to the Christian world at large," the reading of which should be systematically encouraged "in all publick

schools and Universities." He is still aglow with faith in philosophic inquiry and method and results. He is sure, for example, that the Immortality of the Soul is "demonstrable from the knowledge of nature and the light of Reason." He is equally sure that a satisfying philosophical account can be given of every fundamental doctrine of natural and revealed religion.

(3) But in the third stage—starting perhaps from *An Explanation of the Grand Mystery of Godliness* (1660) —there is a change. He begins to put increasing stress on what he finds in Scripture. His philosophical ardour abates, and yields to suspicion of its own worth. He avows his belief that "a greater certainty," even of things demonstrable by natural reason, "is to be drawn from the Scriptures rightly and completely understood than from the clearest fountain of Philosophy." He expresses regret that this discovery had not come to him sooner, since it would certainly "in greatest part have extinguished that so ardent desire of philosophising which seized me when I was very young."

(4) Accordingly, he becomes predominantly a student of the Scriptures, or, to be exact, of their prophetic and apocalyptic portions (Ezekiel, Daniel, the Book of Revelation), as to which he preaches an undoubting assurance that he has found the key to all their difficulties.

"That most clear and distinct understanding of these Prophetical Visions did not happen to me as it were at once, but I attained to the knowledge of these things rather occasionally than by design. Nor am I conscious to myself that I affected this sort of skill, but almost whether I would or no, it instilled itself into me, with so great easiness and perspicuity that I could not, in a manner, but certainly and fully understand those things which others will have to appear so very obscure and uncertain to themselves."

So confident is he of having found the key, that he quietly challenges "any man in his wits, who reads his exposition, without prejudice, to deny that it hath not a certainty plainly mathematical." [1]

(5) A middle point in his progress (or regress) is marked by the *Enchiridion metaphysicum* which came out in 1671, with a dedication to Sheldon, Archbishop of Canterbury (1663–77). More, it appears, had been at Lambeth; and, in talk with Sheldon, had found him disposed to look upon the new "free method of philosophising" with far from unfriendly sentiments—provided always "that the faith, the peace, the institutions of the Church were not thereby menaced." More agreed, and is careful to point out in his treatise the instances in which the experiments of natural science, carried on under the auspices of the recently founded Royal Society (1663), tended rather to strengthen than impair the presumptive evidence for the supernatural. This tallies, of course, with his earlier standpoint; but he discloses the change which has come over him, when, in the Address to the Reader, he turns his back on Descartes whom he had hailed with extravagant praise twenty-five years before. Now he questions the truth of much which he had welcomed in the new Philosophy. Nay, he goes farther, and speaks of Cartesianism as in the highest degree inimical to the principles of religious belief; styles its author the chief of the Nullibists; seems to gloat over some instances of misconception on the part of Des-

[1] Preface to *Grand Mystery of Godliness* (1660).

cartes with respect to natural processes, which More had detected; in short, makes it clear that he has joined the growing party of reaction.[1] And the explanation is not far to seek. What had happened was what could not fail to happen. In his eagerness to defend revealed religion, he had drifted into a reliance on spurious, or at least sensational, forms of the supernatural; and so he renounced Descartes because his clear and cool intellectualism afforded him no foothold or encouragement in this direction. We can see that, for the same reason, he drifted away also from the proper standpoint of his Cambridge friends. In Whichcote there is no trace of any appeal to prophetic mysteries, or occultism, or astrology, or witchcraft, or ghosts as proof of the supernatural. There is barely a trace of it in John Smith[2]; and not much, if any, in Cudworth beyond that *Dissertation on the Seventy Weeks* which possibly a secret doubt of its truth, or value, led him to withhold from the light. In fact, these three remained loyal to the purely rational principle with which they set out, and, therefore, by these the school must be judged. But More, on the intellectual side, went his own way—the way of his temperament—the way of a subjectivism which was not very different from that enthusiasm which he so decried in others. And in this he was inconsistent even with himself—with that deeper faith in Reason as "the

---

[1] Cp. Letter to the Reader in *Divine Dialogues* (1668).

[2] The nearest approach to it is in his sermon on "A Christian's Conflicts and Conquests . . .," a discourse delivered in Huntingdon "where one of Queens' College, in every year on March 25th, is to preach a sermon against witchcraft, diabolical contracts, etc." He just glances at his special topic in the last few sentences and then simply to condemn "their use of any arts, rites or ceremonies, not understood, of which we can give no rational or Divine account."

master light of all his seeing" which really held and
moulded him to the last, and made a mystic of him.
His aberrations were all, so to speak, on the surface of
his mind. They belonged to the fanciful and emotional
stratum of it. They did not express its central life. They
conflicted with that life, and might for a time gain the
upper hand. But only for a time. His essentially rational
self, sooner or later, redressed the balance; and could
do so because his love of the simple truth never failed,
his longing to walk in its light never failed, his faith in
the fellowship of love as a medium of truth never failed.

We have the means of illustrating these statements
in an episode which is both interesting in itself and may
help to round off his personal story.

It has been remarked above that More seldom left
Cambridge for any length of time. No other place had
for him an equal charm—no other, except one. This other
was Ragley, the seat of Edward, Viscount Conway,[1]
situated at the south-west corner of Warwickshire, in
the parish of Arrow. Here More stayed for days, weeks,
or even months, whenever he wished. Here he was free
to live and move as he liked.

And here, amid what he describes as "the solemnness
of the place, its shady walks and hills and woods," where
he lost sight of the world and the world of him, he composed more than one of his most important works.[2]
His connection with it came through Lady Conway,

---

[1] As third Viscount he succeeded his father in June 1655 (see
Rawdon Papers, p. 188). He is better known perhaps as Jeremy
Taylor's admirer and patron. In 1679 he was created the first
Earl of Conway.

[2] "Some of his treatises," e.g. *Conjectura Cabbalistica* (1653),
"were expressly owing to Lady Conway's own desire or
instigation." Ward, p. 202.

who, as Miss Anne Finch, daughter of Sir Henry Finch and sister of Lord Heneage Finch,[1] had been More's pupil at Cambridge.[2] Her marriage to Lord Conway in February 1657 did not interrupt her friendship with More. For his lordship also admired him, and is said to have declared that he kept "everything of the Doctor's with as much reverence as if it was Socrates'."[3] Hence it was natural that Ragley should be open to him—the more so since Lady Conway still regarded herself as his pupil, and still pursued the studies which were their mutual delight. She had learnt to read (in Latin) both Plato and Plotinus. These she continued to read, together with "the abstrusest writers of theosophy." It seems to have been her chief interest in life to investigate and discuss metaphysical subjects. She and More, therefore, could not fail to be good company to each other. Their friendship was, in the most literal sense, Platonic. They talked Plato, or the things for which Plato was supposed to stand, whenever they met; and, for some eight years or so, they met for this purpose pretty often. Then, however, there came a change—a change due to the state of her health. For many years [4] she had suffered from severe headaches, partly a result of her severe and assiduous studies. One imagines that the best cure

[1] Afterwards Earl of Nottingham, Chancellor and Lord Keeper under Charles II.

[2] Her brother, Dr. John Finch, was also a pupil of More's (see *Worthington's Diary*, June 21, 1661, vol. i., p. 339). Ward (p. 289) quotes a letter dated Kensington, February 11, 1651, from Miss Finch to More. It contains queries suggested by reading More's poem on the "Pre-existence of the Soul," and his answer, covering nineteen pages, is also given (pp. 291–310). This points back to a date before 1650 for the beginning of their acquaintance.

[3] Ward, p. 193.

[4] She was troubled in this way for some years before More became acquainted with her. Ward, p. 204.

would have been to give up her studies and live much in the open air. But she did neither. We are told that in the interval of her attacks she ever went back with all eagerness to her speculations; but we hear nothing of her living in the open air, or even of her leaving the house. Indeed, one gets the impression that she became more and more of a recluse—driven back upon herself by extreme pain, which grew at last to be chronic and almost unbearable. There were times when she could not see even her husband. Thus in a letter dated 30 October, 1666, Lord Conway writes: "This is the first I have written to you since my arrival in England, for at Ragley I met nothing but the sad condition of my wife, whom I could not see all the while I was there, though I stayed a fortnight." [1]

We gather that the situation was rather a dreary one for his lordship, and it is not surprising to find him betaking himself to the gaieties of the Court at Whitehall. [2]

[1] *Rawdon Papers*, p. 219.

Readers of *John Inglesant* may recall Lady Cardiff, the wealthy "peeress in her own right," "carefully educated" and "learned in many languages," who had her "principal seat at Oulton in Dorsetshire," and married Eustace Inglesant, and collected around her "eccentrics, as they were called," including "Von Helmont the great alchemist," and Dr. Henry More of Cambridge, and Quakers (chap. ix.). Her husband speaks of her "headaches," and his exclusion from her society by the state of her health, or by Quacks and Quakers; and, in the end, is assassinated by an Italian who obtains access to Oulton by professing Quakerism (chap. xv.). Mr. Shorthouse often quotes word for word from Lord Conway's letters to Sir George Rawdon, or from Ward, or from More (chap. xvii.): so it is clear that he had the Conways and Ragley in mind. But, as over against his "romance," in which the lady at any rate fares badly, the plain facts seem to be those narrated in the text.

[2] See *Rawdon Papers*, Letter 96, p. 221 (30 October, 1666); Letter 99, p. 228 (8 January, 1666–7); Letter 100, p. 231 (29 October, 1667), etc.

But he appears to have done what he could for the sufferer. He allowed, if he did not invite, Baron von Helmont (son of Jean Baptist von Helmont, the famous chemist) to take up his abode at Ragley and act as her physician. But under him she grew worse rather than better; and no wonder, considering that in his treatment of her he was guided by "occult medical studies," which the patient was encouraged to share with him.

Either before this, or afterwards, she [1] went to France, in order that her cranium might be opened; but the French surgeons declined to operate, though they ventured to make incisions in the jugular arteries.

Hereupon, or possibly at an earlier date, Lord Conway induced her to try an experiment from which he himself had great hopes. Writing to his brother-in-law, Sir George Rawdon, at Dublin on 26 July, 1665, he says "the chief business" of his letter was to entreat Sir George to prevail with Mr. Valentine Greatrex,[2] of Youghall, in Munster, to come over to his wife. For Mr. Greatrex is "said to cure all diseases by the touch, or stroking of the hand." All reports of his skill represent it as so great that he wonders Sir George makes no

[1] There is an entry in the Diary of Henry Townshend of Elmley Lovett (1640–1663) which points to an early date—too early, indeed, if Lord Conway was not married before Feb. 1657. The entry is as follows (p. 33), July 1656: "Lord Conway taken going into France to see his lady, who is sick." One can only conclude that the reference is to Lord Conway's father, who died at Paris on 26 June, 1655; and that the diarist is wrong in his date. (See *Rawdon Papers*, p. 185, note.) Letter 84 (in these papers), of date 12 October, 1658, throws considerable light on Lady Conway's case.

[2] For Greatrex or Greatrakes, see *D.N.B.* and references there given. The name is variously spelt. Greatrex seems to have been the more usual.

mention of it. For his own part, he is of opinion that his wife is "very unlikely to receive help any other way," and Dr. More, who is at Ragley,[1] agrees with him. He is urgent, therefore, that the "stroker" should come over to Bristol, "where my horses shall meet him and bring him hither." From another letter, dated 9 February, 1666, we learn that Greatrex had been at Ragley for a fortnight; that he had taken great pains with Lady Ragley; that he was very affectionate to do all that lay in his power; but that, so far, he had failed. At the end of a third week he had still failed; and then left for London. The probability is that the lady had no faith or too little faith. But, if so, she differed from her husband. Lord Conway's faith had been more confirmed. "I must confess" (he says) "that before his arrival I did not believe the tenth part of those things which I have been an eye-witness of." There is indeed nothing miraculous in the matter, he is sure; but a wonderful "sanative virtue" which lies in the agent, and flows out of him. Not that it extends to all diseases. The report to that effect is a mistake. There are cases which are beyond him; and Lady Conway's is of this number. There are others which he cannot dispatch without "a great deal of pains." But most of the cases seem easy to him, and are of a manifold description—including even a case of leprosy.

After Greatrex's futile visit the curtain drops on Lady Conway and her afflictions for ten years. Then,

[1] Dr. George Rust, Dean of Connor, and later (from 1667), Bishop of Dromore—Jeremy Taylor's friend—was also at Ragley, and of the same mind. His *Discourse of Truth* (edited and published by Joseph Glanvill in 1682) connects him with the Cambridge men, particularly with Cudworth, of whose doctrines the *Discourse* is an echo.

on 28 December, 1677, Lord Conway writes from Ragley to Sir George Rawdon: "In my family all the women about my wife, and most of the rest, are Quakers, and Mons. Van Helmont is governor of that flock, an un-pleasing sort of people, silent, sullen, and of a reserved conversation. . . . These and all of that society have free access to my wife; but I believe Dr. More, though he was in the house all the last summer, did not see her above twice or thrice." Ragley, in fact, was no fit place for Sir George's young daughter, whom he was about to send into England. It had become a gloomy habitation —repellent to himself and no less so to Dr. More. For the latter especially the change deprived Ragley of its charm. To quote his biographer—"This unexpected scene at Ragley . . . affected him so much at length that he received the account of it with tears and labour'd all that a Faithful Friend could do to set the Lady right, as to her judgment in these matters."

More than seventeen years before he had expressed [1] his vehement dislike of the Familists and Quakers above any other sects, "because he took them for no sect of *Christians* at all but a total Apostasy from Christianity"; and, in this sweeping condemnation, he had carried Lady Conway with him. But now she had changed her mind; and had done so, it would seem, as the result of personal experience. First she had been led—we cannot tell how—to "change some of her servants for Quakers," and from this change had reaped more benefit than from all the doctors. They were so quiet and restful. In answer to More's remonstrance she wrote: "The weight of my affliction lies so heavy upon me that 'tis incredible how

[1] In Preface to *Grand Mystery of Godliness* (1660).

very seldom I can endure anyone in my chamber, but I find them to be so still, quiet, and serious that the company of such will be very acceptable to me." No doubt through her new servants she heard the story of Quaker sufferings, and was "much refreshed by the account of their trials and consolations." So she concluded "that they were fitted, from the sundry and heavy exercises that themselves had experimented, and their patience and supports under them, to administer comfort to others in great distress." Her Quaker friends had no power to drive away her pains. During her last years frequent fits intensified them to the point of torment. But they could impart to her the secret of peace; and this was much. It was vain, therefore, for the good doctor "to labour all that a faithful friend could, to set her right." She had the witness in herself. When he argued that their very name [1] was against them, she wrote: "I was never in love with the name of Quaker nor their 'Rusticity,' and only regarded their Principles and Practises so far as they were good and christian." [2] When, again, he brought up his old objection to the Quakers as people condemned by their origin from the Familists, she replied that some Quakers may have been Familists, but not all, or many. Certainly "George Fox was never listed into that sect before his taking up this Form." Then she goes on—"I am of your opinion that there are many bad people amongst them as well as of other Professions, and do also believe that their converse with you might be of good use to them, for the

[1] In the *Discourse of Enthusiasm*, p. 25, he says that such deluded souls take Quaking "to be an infallible sign that they are actuated by the Spirit of God."
[2] Ward, p. 197.

Effigies HENRICI MORI Cantabrigiensis S.T.D. Ætat. 65

HENRY MORE
From a print by David Loggan.

clearing up of their understanding and advancing their progress towards the best things; and, therefore, that your conversation with them at London might be—as you express it—charitably intended, like that of a Physician frequenting his Patients, for the encrease or confirmation of their health. But I must profess that my converse with them is to receive health and refreshment from them. I pray God to give us all a clear discerning between melancholy enthusiasm and true inspiration, that we may not be imposed to believe a lye." [1]

More, it seems, proposed to interview some of the Quaker leaders in London. He would do so in the rôle of a spiritual physician, and his friend has not lost faith in his healing touch. But, for her own part, she finds their touch no less healing and refreshing than his own. May God give him and her and all concerned ability to see the truth! More surely must have felt the Christian grace of this attitude. Did he also feel its delicate, not to say satirical, hint of remonstrance?

More had his meeting in London with "the best and chiefest of the Quakers," including R. B., i.e. Robert Barclay; W. P., i.e. William Penn; G. K., i.e. George Keith, and "their great leader (as most account of him) George Fox." [2] Fox, if not the others, repelled More; but he did not repel Lady Conway. In the following year, when at the extremity of her suffering, she sent for him; and he came at once. The entry in his *Journal*

[1] Ward, p. 199.

[2] Probably in November or December 1677: and it seems to have had no good result. What More thought of the others is not recorded, but concerning Fox he is reported to have said that "in conversing with him he felt himself as it were turned into brass. . . ."

M

gives the impression that he turned out of his way to come. Her summons found him at Worcester, or perhaps at Pershore or Evesham, early in March 1678, and he writes: "I . . . struck to Ragley in Warwickshire to visit the Lady Conway, who I understood was very desirous to see me, and whom I found tender and loving and willing to detain me longer than I had freedom to stay." It is a safe inference that he was a means of grace to her. Within a year of his visit she died—23 February, 1679—and was buried on 17 April at the parish church of Arrow. The reason for so unusual a delay was this— "Her husband was absent in Ireland at the time of her decease, but in order that he might have a last look at her features, Van Helmont preserved the body in spirits of wine and placed it in a coffin with a glass over the face."

In his *Grand Mystery of Godliness* More occupies seven chapters with a refutation of Familism and its supposed offspring Quakerism; and defends his so large treatment of so small a subject on the ground that the subject is by no means small—because "the mystery of Familism and I doubt of Quakerism is the worst of all heresies, viz., the utter rejecting of the Person of Christ as to His humane nature, with all His offices assigned to Him by His Father." This was written "from my study at Christ's College, Cambridge, on June 12, 1660."

Four years earlier (1656),[1] in a letter under the nom-de-plume of "Mastix" (scourge) he had made the same charge, and had urged that this evil leaven of Quakerism might be all the more diabolic as being wrought by Satan through men and women, some of whom were conspicuous

[1] Ward, p. 201.

for great severity of life and self-mortification and close adherence to what they called the light within. Seven years later (1667), in the fifth of his *Divine Dialogues* (p. 459) he renewed the charge; but in the second edition of that book (1678) he added a long note (pp. 565–575) in which he confessed a change of mind. He had been reading Robert Barclay's *Apology* (of which the English edition appeared in that year), and had come across pronouncements which had given him the greatest satisfaction. After quoting at length four places where Barclay expounds what More considered the truth about the relation of the historic to the inward Christ, he says: "These are golden words indeed and the very index or touchstone of the true and pure gold." He is glad to find himself mistaken, and to find it true, as he had once foretold of the more sincere Quakers, that "those who persist in a serious and sincere desire of this sort of knowledge which tends to life and godliness will at last turn safe to Jesus Christ, the only Great Shepherd and Bishop of their souls." His only further wish for the Quakers is that they will now "carefully wipe off" all filthy remnants of Familism; and come forth in their own "honest countenance."

In fact, as soon as the mask—largely of his own fancying—fell away from the face of Quakerism, More began to realise that he had no quarrel with it. Nor is this at all surprising if we glance at his own religious history and experience. "Even in my childhood"—he says—"an inward sense of the Divine presence was so strong upon my mind that I did then believe there could no deed, word, or thought be hidden from Him; nor was I by others, that were older than myself, to be otherwise persuaded." He speaks of this deep religious feeling as an innate sense or notion. Might he not, with equal fitness, have called it an inner light? His father was a Calvinist, and he was taught the Calvinistic doctrine of predestination. But he could never "swallow" it. And one day, "in a ground belonging to Eton College," he came to this resolve—"if I am one of those that are predestinated into hell, where all things are full of nothing but cursing and blasphemy, yet will I behave myself there patiently and submissively towards God; and if there be any one thing more than another that is acceptable to Him, *that* will I set myself to do with a sincere heart and to the utmost of my power. Being certainly persuaded that if I thus demeaned myself, He would hardly keep me long in that place." "Though He slay me, yet will I trust Him"—what but the inner light led a boy of fifteen to so Job-like a confidence in the justice of God? At Cambridge, as a result of immersing himself "over head and ears" for four years in philosophic studies, he fell into a sort of scepticism— not, as he carefully tells us, regarding the existence of God, or the duties of morality—"for of these he never had the least doubt"—but regarding the origin and end of life. "He was puzzled, like many a young dreamer before him, as to the meaning of existence and what were its shows and what its substance."

Nor did his mental confusion pass away until he began to realise clearly what became thenceforth the central conviction of his life—viz. that the highest knowledge is won not merely, or mainly, by the study of things, but by "the purgation of the mind from all sorts of vices whatsoever." In other words, there must be the pure heart before there can be a clear vision of the highest truth. He learned this lesson partly from the Platonic writers with whom at this stage he made acquaintance, and, most of all, from "that golden little book with which Luther is also said to have been wonderfully taken—the *Theologia Germanica.*"

Hereupon there arose in him a violent conflict between "the Divine principle and the animal nature," or, as Paul would say, the flesh and the spirit—a conflict which issued for him in a new birth. He felt "the Divine seed alone is that which is acceptable unto God, and the sole invincible basis of all true religion." His former "insatiable desire and thirst after the knowledge of things" became almost wholly extinguished. He became "solicitous about nothing so much as a more full union with the divine and celestial principle, the inward flowing well-spring of life eternal—with the most fervent prayers breathing often unto God that He would be pleased thoroughly to set him free from the dark chains and sordid captivity of his own will." And no sooner, strangely, had he entered upon this course, and his immoderate desire after mere knowledge been allayed, than he began to have a clearer assurance of those very things which he had desired to know. Gradually light as well as peace came to him. "Within a few years" he "got into a most joyous and lucid state of mind"— the very opposite of his former state.

Is not this substantially a description of the experience to which the Friends bore witness? Is not the language even partly the same? And what could come nearer to their sense, or meaning, than the two mottoes he adopted about the same time—*Claude fenestras ut luceat Domus* and *Amor Dei lux animae*? To light the house of the soul close the windows of sense; and, the soul's light is the love of God. He professed to have received these mottoes from a venerable old man with whom he walked and talked in a dream—one being concealed in a silver, and the other in a golden key. Anyhow, these were the keys by means of which he actually found his way into mystic fellowship with God and His truth. It was his habit—like the Quakers—often to withdraw from the world of sense into himself as into a holy temple, that there he might listen for the voice of God, and cherish upon the altar of his heart the love of God.

But note here an important point. The voice of God for which he listened in this spiritual temple was never other than the voice of Reason. For the voice of God which spoke to him must be the voice of truth; and how could truth be perceived except by Reason? Reason, in fact, is just the organ in man to which truth addresses itself; and apart from which he cannot know whether truth is speaking or not. Therefore (changing the figure), to despise Reason is simply to despise and destroy the light by which truth can alone be recognised. It was to act, as More himself says, like a company of men who, travelling by night, "with links, torches, and lanterns," put out their borrowed light from misconceit of it in comparison with "the sweet and cheerful splendour of the day"; and choose rather "to foot it in the dark and tumble into the next ditch" than to go happily forward with such light as they had. His quarrel with the enthusiasts—among whom he thought there was good ground to reckon the Quakers—was that they refused to see this, but prated of an inner light *above* Reason which put a sanction upon things evil or foolish, and called them divine. Nevertheless even here he was implicitly at one with them. For what at least the intelligent Quaker wanted to express was his consciousness of an insight more immediate and simple and convincing than that of reason. Reason he took to be the same as reasoning, and its insight the outcome of a logical process—whereas the truth most clear and dear to his own consciousness was such as he could not prove, nor which ever could be proved. And More did not question this. Nay, he agreed that there are ranges of truth which Reason in its natural state, or in the unnatural state to which it has been reduced by sin, cannot see. But let the heart be cleansed by the operation of the Holy Spirit; and, with the heart, the Reason also is cleansed—is cleared and exalted and irradiated, and becomes what he calls a *Divine Sagacity* which can see, as in a flash, or a stream of light, the truth as it is in Jesus. Consequently the organ of truth is never anything else than Reason, just as the organ of sight in the body, however dull or keen, is never anything else than the eye. In a word, the inner light is always the effect of a rational response to truth, whether the response comes in a flash of insight or a reasoned process. But, as regards the highest truths especially, you must be pure of heart if you would be clear of head, or if Reason is to function at its best. Was not this, in part, the message of Fox and Barclay?

CHAPTER VII

PETER STERRY (*d.* 1672)

Mysticism in full bloom

PETER STERRY was a native of Surrey, and entered Emmanuel College, Cambridge, on 21 October, 1629. Nothing is known of his parentage; but the fact that he went to Emmanuel points to a Puritan home, and the fact that he went as a sizar [1] seems to imply some degree of poverty. After graduating B.A. in 1633, he was elected Fellow in 1636, and proceeded M.A. the year following. This is proof enough of his scholarship. For the rest, our light on his university career is limited to the statement that he and "one Sadler were the first who were observed to make a public profession of Platonism." If we remember that Benjamin Whichcote had entered the college three years before Sterry (1626), became Fellow in 1633, and Tutor as well as Fellow in 1634, we can guess the medium of Sterry's Platonism.

Sterry had a natural affinity with the new influence, and might be expected to take the lead in yielding himself ardently to it. By temperament he was a mystic, if a mystic may be described as a man absorbed in the study or experience of God. At the same time, he was a Calvinist; and he did not cease to be a Calvinist when he became a Platonist. There is a link between Calvinism

---

[1] See Mullinger, ii. 252.

and Platonism, in that both endeavour to conceive and construe the universe from the standpoint of the Divine nature. The difference between them may be said to lie in their view of the Divine character. Sterry's Platonism led him, while allowing full scope to the power and justice and wisdom of God, to put the goodness of God first and last. This was a new phenomenon in Puritanism.

When he left Cambridge is not clear; but he settled in London some time before May, 1643, when he was one of the fourteen divines nominated by the House of Lords for the Westminster Assembly. Though he seems to have taken little part in its debates, and is found on none of its committees, he was still a member in September 1646, and marked as a "notorious Independent,"[1] and a "zealous and firm advocate to the Parliament." This would recommend him to Lord Brook, to whose wife (after his death in Lichfield fight, 1642) he became chaplain in 1644. His association with Sir Harry Vane is revealed by his being examined, near the same time, about a plot in which the latter was suspected to have a hand. At least from November 1645, he was an occasional preacher before the House of Commons or Lords. For on the 26th of that month—"the solemn day of their monthly fast"—he preached from the text, John xvi. 8, and presently published his sermon under the title, "The Spirit convincing of Sinne." He tells "the Honourable Knights and Burgesses that his one desire had been so to speak as that their souls, counsels, wars may be carried on by the Spirit of God Who, in the language of the Scriptures, is not only the Dove for

---

[1] Along with Philip Nye and others; see *Athenæ Oxon.* iii. 912. In this respect, of course, he was not a follower of Whichcote; but he cared just as little for "forms."

Purity and Peace, but also the true Eagle for Wisdom and Power." Very heart-searching was the preacher's application of his theme; and one hopes that Cromwell was there. He, at any rate, would relish the doctrine, however "high-pitched" might be some of the expressions in which it was set forth. Sir Benjamin Rudyard styled his preaching "too high for this world and too low for the other." Cromwell's appreciation of him was instinctive. The mystic strain which repelled a clear-cut dialectician like Richard Baxter attracted the Protector. Baxter associated him with Sir Harry Vane and questioned "whether vanity [1] and sterility had ever been more happily conjoined."

Sterry's sermons were seldom doctrinal in the current sense of the term. They were always concerned with the deep things of the Spirit, and with these as directly related to their manifestation in the events of the time. Every victory or defeat in the great fight of the people for what he believed to be the cause of justice and liberty was to him an operation of the "Spirit," and a sign of His approval or disapproval—a call to repentance or thanksgiving.[2] Cromwell saw this so vividly that he

[1] But he lived to change his mind. Writing in 1675 Baxter says of Sterry: "Doubtless his head was strong, his wit admirably pregnant, his searching studies hard and sublime, and, I think, his heart replenished with holy love to God, and great charity, moderation and peaceableness towards man: Insomuch that I heartily repent that I so far believed fame as to think somewhat hardlier and less charitably of him and his few adherents than I now hope they did deserve. *Hasty judgment* and *believing fame* is a cause of unspeakable hurt to the world, and injury to our brethren" (*Catholic Theology* (1675), Bk. ii. pt. 3, p. 107). Baxter wrote thus after reading the Preface to Sterry's posthumous book on *The Freedom of the Will*.

[2] See, e.g., page 7 of his sermon on the "Clouds in which Christ comes."—Rev. i. 7; Oct. 27, 1647 (preached before the House of Commons).

wondered why men should look for any other, or clearer, outward "sign." To them both History, made or in the making, contained the living word of God. Hence it was natural that the two should draw together; and that, in due time, the preacher should be appointed one of the Lord General's chaplains-in-ordinary (July 1649). He had to preach at Whitehall or Hampton Court on Sundays, and every Thursday morning at the former. He had (for some months) been a Preacher to the Council of State at a salary of £100 a year. With his chaplaincy the allowance was doubled; and he had lodgings in Whitehall.

Tolerance of varying religious opinions sprang at once out of Sterry's intensely spiritual faith; and it is easy to see that a like faith on Cromwell's part inspired the well-nigh unlimited tolerance for which he was conspicuous. Sterry was the preacher when "the High Court of Parliament" met in St. Margaret's, Westminster, on 5 November, 1651, to render thanks for the "crowning mercy" at Worcester on 3 September; and it was Cromwell's voice, no doubt, which had nominated him for this distinction. He celebrated the occasion as "England's deliverance from the Northern Presbytery compared with a deliverance from the Roman Papacy"; and no loftier plea, if regard be had to the grounds of it, could have been urged on behalf of spiritual freedom. He had no quarrel with Presbyterianism in itself. In the dedication to this sermon he speaks of the Scottish Church as that which, in his opinion, possesses almost the purest form of government. But the attitude of the Presbyterians, both in Scotland and England, towards differing forms had entered like iron into his soul; and had driven him to the conclusion that, if anything, they

were worse foes to liberty than the Papists. The corruption of the best turns to the worst; and the same
Anti-Christian temper which rules in the Papacy (he
says) becomes fuller of "dispute and danger" in the
purer form of Presbytery, because it is then fuller of
"mystery," i.e. more subtle and concealed in its working.
And what is the specifically Anti-Christian temper? It is,
to value unduly the form (of a Church or a doctrine) in
such wise as to make it a bar between a man and his
brethren, or between the soul and its living Lord; and
so "fetter" the sweet "outgoings" of the Spirit. Cromwell must have felt his soul refreshed that day.

A few sentences may suffice for further details of his
life. His mysticism does not seem to have made him
unpractical. He was a man of affairs. He is seen making
an inventory of the State Records (1653–1654). He
reports on some works in MS. which the Council have
a mind to purchase; he examines Archbishop Usher's
library, and advises what part of it might be bought by
the State; he acts as one of the "Triers" and (possibly)
as assistant Latin Secretary under Milton. In 1655 he
sits in the Conference intended by the Protector to
open the way for admission of the Jews to citizenship;
and was (we may be sure) not one of the clerical majority
who crossed the project.

Cromwell's death (3 September, 1658) threw him into
the shade. He retired to Hackney; took pupils to eke out
his means of livelihood; preached, as he could, to "a
gathered people"; and was one of the first for whom a
licence was obtained under the Indulgence Act of 1672.[1]

---

[1] It was granted at the instance of Edward Bushell (on 16 May)
for services to be held at his house at Homerton or Little St.

On 1 November following he died—"full of those joys"
(says his editor) "in which he was taken up"; and
testifying that "it then pleased God to give him full
assurance of those truths he had taught to others." To
his enemies he was a "blasphemer," a "Parasite," one
who always kept "on that side of the hedge which has
proved trump." To those who knew him best he was
an object of wonder and affection. One of these [1] speaks
particularly of the "fulness of his thought which seemed
to overflow and to be never straitened—howsoever the
subjects he engaged in—although strength of body often
failed him."

Another [2] dares not venture to speak, so great is his
"love and veneration" lest he should "offend against the
Spring while commending the Stream." He will, therefore, merely say that "our author was indeed a true father
in Christ, and so esteemed by all who knew him: for his
own great understanding and experience in Divine things;

Helen's (see article on the Bushells of Frodsham, in *Transactions
of Congregational Historical Society*, vol. vi. No. 5). Bushell was
distantly related to Sterry (ibid., p. 380). Sterry is named a
Presbyterian, but this proves nothing. Nearly all Nonconformists
were apt to be called Presbyterians.

[1] Preface to his volume of sermons entitled *The Appearance
of God to Man.* . . .

[2] Preface to a second volume of sermons entitled *The Rise,
Race and Royalty of the Kingdom of God.* Whichcote was "once
in conversation with Sterry on some obscure points in Divinity,"
when "he explained himself with such ease and clearness that
the doctor, rising from his seat and embracing him, exclaimed:
'Peter, thou hast overcome me, thou art all pure intellect'; and
when news of Sterry's death was brought to him he said in
surprise and great concern: 'Well, as much as the World thinks
me to love money, I tell thee I should be well contented to part
with half of what I have to obtain only some hours' free conversation with that greatly enlightened Friend of ours who is now
taken from us': or to that effect." He was, also, willing to preach
his funeral sermon; but it does not appear that he did.

for the excellency of his ministry—whereby he did in
Jesus Christ, through the Gospel, beget and edify many;
as also for the great tenderness and father-like bowels
which, throughout his whole ministry and in all his other
converses, he delighted to be still expressing towards all
the weak and little ones. Nor was his skill herein less
considerable than his naturalness." He was "still careful
to provide milk" for the babes whilst setting stronger
meat before the man.[1]

II

Sterry's theology, in many respects, is defiant of
system. It is the product of a mind which often lets
itself go on the wings of a too exuberant fancy, or is
driven along by a rush of poetic sentiment. Hence his
arguments are very apt to be interwoven of imagery
which, however beautiful, yields no rational meaning.
He is woefully lacking in self-criticism. His metaphysics
are a bad specimen of that *a priori* philosophy which
ran riot before Locke, or even Descartes. He never
defines with "his eye on the object," but always with
reference to some assumed principle of deductive
thought. His idea of personality, e.g. both in God and
man, is the quintessence of vagueness; and quite power-
less to hold him back from that gulf of Pantheism into
which he certainly had no wish to fall. Moreover, his

[1] It is a curious comment on Baillie's report (*Letters*, ii. 429)
that Sterry lost favour after Cromwell's death, when we read
of his being chosen to conduct prayers in the House of Commons
on the four Wednesdays of February 1659, also on Saturday the
28th, followed by Wednesdays 23rd and 30th March, April 6th
and Friday 22nd. In each case the entry is "Mr. Sterry prayed."
Hist. MSS., New Series, vol. iv., pp. 522–567.

Puritan reverence for the Scriptures as, throughout, the infallible Word of God committed him to the hopeless task of discovering, for all his statements, some textual support, and to an allegorical method of interpretation which (as usual) drew out of the text just what it liked to put in; while a natural desire not to break too abruptly with orthodox phraseology constrained him, not seldom, to press his thoughts into categories to which they had no real relation. He felt bound to be logical; but his soul was lyrical and impatient of logic. Spiritual intuitions of a mystic striving for expression through an intractable mass of conventional formulæ, is the picture he suggests. Having said this, however, it can be added that the general drift and cardinal features of his theology are perfectly clear.

Thus (a) its Calvinism appears in the absoluteness of the place assigned to God. God is Being—all Being. Will is the essence of His being. Everything is the direct effect of His will. There are, in truth, no real secondary causes. There is, strictly speaking, no will besides His; and freedom of will, if by freedom is meant a power to choose or act independently of God, is absurd. "The will of man in every motion, act and determination of it, is from eternity predetermined in the divine under-standing, as in its first cause and original." "The connection, the dependence between God and the creature—the first, the universal Cause and every Effect—is much more universal, intimate, immediate, inseparable than that between any effect and any second cause. We have a demonstration to our sense from the interposal of a Cloud between our eyes and a clear Sky, that the beams are continued streams of light from the body of the Sun. In that moment in which they cease to flow from the Sun, to subsist in the Sun, they cease to be." [1]

(b) The distinctly Christian element appears in the central place assigned to Christ. The Godhead is a Trinity of Life, Light and Love. Life is identified with the Father. Love is identified with the Spirit as the informing soul of the Father and the Son. Light is identified with the Son. The Son is the "mind of God," is the "Treasury of all ideas." [2] He is His Wisdom, or His image. The last is Sterry's favourite comparison. The Son is at once the first Image of God, "the clearest and fullest effulgency or brightness of all His glories in His own most proper and most glorious form" [3]; and, "in that, the FIRST image of the whole Creation and of every creature, as a part of the whole." Thus, the Son "standeth in the middle between God and all creatures, comprehending both entirely in one, in Himself." [4] He is also the "Way by which God descendeth into the Creature, by which the Creation cometh forth from God." As such, He could become manifest in flesh; and did so in "our Lord Jesus Christ." The incarnation was nothing strange, nor was the Fall which occasioned it. The Fall, with all its seeming miseries, was due to the act of God. God, for His greater glory, withdrew Himself from man ("as it were a handbreadth off"), turned away His face, deprived man's understanding of its proper light. This left him to the "shadowy images" of a darkened world. These Images, as so many will-o'-the-wisps, deluded his will into mistaking and choosing and

---

[1] *Discourse of the Freedom of the Will* (1675), p. 63, etc.
[2] Ibid., p. 200.   [3] Ibid., p. 49.   [4] Ibid., p. 198.

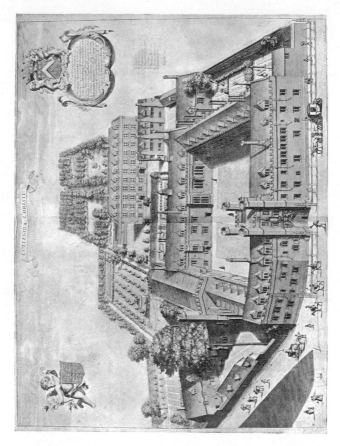

CHRIST'S COLLEGE, CAMBRIDGE
From a print by David Loggan.

embracing the false for the true. So, "the soul sinks into the depth of darkness, in which darkness it springs up, the same moment, into evils of Sin, Deformity, Death, Wrath, Torment." [1]

Nevertheless, all is well. The soul's descent has been attended and shared by Christ. "We are sojourners together in *His land*. He suffers in all our sufferings. *He is in all things made like* unto us, sin only excepted." [2] In human form He drew upon Himself all the "contrariety" of human sin, and submitted to "all extremities of suffering." At the same time, He so identified Himself with man in his sin that He drew upon Himself the whole force of that divine wrath against sin which is only an aspect of divine love—love "disguising itself" behind a "fury" which has the destruction of sin for its object. And by this sacrifice to the holiness of God the destruction was achieved. "Jesus, the supreme harmony, the everlasting Righteousness, by dying, carries the descent of things to the lowest point. He makes an end of Sin, Sufferings, Wrath and Death for ever, by the dissolution and end of the seat, the subject of all these, viz. the shadowy Image. . . . The death of Jesus Christ is as the midnight of things. The *Sun* of the eternal Image and glory, having by its course, in the shadowy Image, touched the *utmost bounds of distance* from itself, now begins to return to itself again." [3]

But Jesus (as Paul says) is essentially spirit.[4] Therefore, " Jesus in His mediatory Kingdom and glory casts off the Vail of Flesh, as from His divine so from His

[1] Ibid., p. 117.
[2] Ibid., p. 130.
N

[2] Ibid., pp. 79, 129.
[4] 2 Cor. iii. 17.

human nature. The days of His flesh are now past. He is a quickening spirit, all spirit and life. His human nature is now all spirit, and, by having the Godhead, hath the Fountain of Spirit and Life in itself." Thus, potentially, Death has been done away. Life alone reigns. In union with the risen Christ the whole is rising —man first, as the head; and, through him, "all the particular forms of things as they stand without man in their own proper existences."[1] In fine, "our Jesus is the great Jubilee, where all debts are remitted, all servants go free, all persons return to their Inheritances, to the free possession, the full fruition of themselves and them. In the Resurrection of the Lord Jesus, from Him, as the root springing up into the Body of the Saints; through them into the rest of the Creation as Branches of the same tree. All sins are pardoned, the whole Creation is set free from its bondage to Vanity and Corruption. All things return to a free fruition of themselves, of all Beauties and Joys in their native Inheritance, their original Images, the proper Ideas in Christ. First Christ; then the Saints; then, through them, Heaven and Earth and the Seas, with all things in them are made new, by being married anew, by being newly re-invested with the Glories of their original."[2]

(c) Accordingly, Sterry's theology—centred in Christ— is a grand Theodicy. In the light of God and His Christ he sees the universe as an emanation proceeding by various stages of darkness and light, from God to God; growing ever more beautiful the more clearly it unfolds; and crowned at last with the outshining glory of ineffable love.

[1] Discourse, p. 131.   [2] Ibid., pp. 132–3.

The language of Bailey's *Festus* might have been his:

> I beheld all things rejoice beneath the light of Love,
> Which seems to burn within us and beam through,
> Lost in the boundless loneliness of God;
> I saw earth's war-scarred countenance sweetly glide
> Into the angel-lineaments of peace:
> And gentlest sorrow dream herself to joy.
> Tears shed on earth were reaped in heaven in smiles
> And what was sown in sighs was reaped in songs.

Here is a passage[1] which finely illustrates his ruling conception; and it is worth quoting for its eloquence:

"A poetical history, or work framed by an excellent spirit, for a Pattern of Wisdom and Worth and Happiness, hath this, as a chief rule, for the contrivance of it, upon which all its Graces and Beauties depend— viz.: that Persons and things be carried to the *utmost extremity*, into a state where they seem altogether incapable of any return to Beauty or Bliss; that then by just degrees of harmonious proportions, they be raised again to a state of highest Joy and Glory. You have examples of this in the divine pieces of those Divine Spirits (as they are esteemed and styled) *Homer, Virgil, Tasso*, our English *Spenser*, with some few others like to these. The works of these persons are called *Poems*. So is the Work of God in Creation and its contrivance from the beginning to the end named ποίημα τοῦ θεοῦ, God's poem. It is an elegant and judicious observation of a

---

[1] Ibid., p. 179. In Sterry's frequent insistence on the emanative principle is traceable his indebtedness to Platonism or rather Neo-Platonism. Another very marked influence is that of Boehme (1575–1621), whose name indeed he does not seem to mention, but with whom much of his thought and phraseology present a very close affinity. Boehme attracted considerable attention in England; see, e.g., Charles Hotham's *Ad Philosophiam Teutonicam* (London, 1648).

learned and holy divine, that the Works of Poets, in
the excellencies of their imaginaton and contrivances,
were imitations drawn from those Original Poems, the
Divine works and contrivances of the Eternal Spirit.
We may by the fairest lights of Reason and Religion
thus judge, that excellent Poets, in the heights of their
fancies and spirits, were touched and warmed with a
Divine Ray through which the supream Wisdom formed
upon them and so upon their work, some weak impression
and obscure Image of itself. Thus it seemeth to be altogether *Divine* that That work shineth in our eyes with
the greatest Beauties; infuseth into our Spirits the
sweetest delights; transporteth us most out of ourselves
unto the kindness and most ravishing touches and
senses of the Divinity, which, diffusing itself through
the amplest Variety, and so to the remotest Distances,
and the most opposed Contrarieties, bindeth up all with
an Harmonious Order into an exact unity; which con-
veyeth things down by a gradual descent to the lowest
Depths and deepest Darknesses; then bringeth them up
again to the highest point of all most flourishing Felici-
ties, opening the *beginning in the end*, espousing the end
to the beginning. This is what Aristotle in his *Discourse
of Poetry* commendeth to us as the most artful and
surprising untying of the knot, διὰ ἀνάγνωσιν or by a
discovery. This is that which Jesus Christ pointeth at
in Himself, who is the Wisdom of God, the Manifold
Wisdom of God, in Whom all the Treasures of Wisdom
and Knowledge lie hid, in whom all the Divine contrivances are formed and perfected. *What will you say,
when you shall see the Son of Man return* there where
He was at first?"

III

Sterry the Theologian exposes many a weak spot to the shafts of criticism. But he stands beyond question when, in virtue of his theology, he urges the old, oft-forgotten lesson that if God is Love, then the Christian law of life is Love. One of the noblest hymns in praise of Love (outside the New Testament) is chanted by Sterry, in magnificent prose, in the Preface to that treatise from which most of our quotations have been drawn. The treatise itself, except for frequent passages and sentences of great beauty, is a chaotic performance; and will be dismissed by any matter-of-fact reader who might conceivably attempt its perusal as "a piece of clotted nonsense." But in the Preface the writer's inmost heart leaps up; and gleams like a stream of purest crystal in the light of that love which he finds supreme in God and commends as supreme for man.

1. "Dear Reader, if thou wouldest be led to that sea which is as the gathering together and confluence of all the Waters of Life, follow the stream of Divine Love as it holdeth on its course, from its head in Eternity through every work of God, through every creature. So shalt thou be not only happy in thine end, but in the way—while this stream of Love shall not only be thy guide by thy side, but shall carry thee along in its soft and delicious bosom, bearing thee up in the bright arms of its own Divine Power, sporting with thee all along, washing thee white as snow in its own pure floods, and bathing thy whole Spirit and Person in heavenly unexpressible sweetness."

2. "Study and practise that great command of Love as the Lesson of thy whole Life, with which alone thou

art to entertain thyself, and all the heavenly Company, both here and in Eternity. Let no differences of Principles or Practices divide thee in thine affection from any person. He who seems to me as a Samaritan to a Jew—most worthy of contempt and hatred, most apt to wound and kill me—may hide under the shape of a Samaritan, a generous, affectionate Neighbour, Brother and Friend. When I lie wounded and dying, neglected by those who are nearest to me, most esteemed by me, this person may pour Oil and Wine into my Wounds, with tender and constant care, at his own expense, bring me back to life and joy. How evident it hath been in the History of all times, that in Parties most remote one from the other, most opposed one to the other, Persons have been found of equal excellencies in all kinds, of equal integrity to Truth and Goodness. Our most Orthodox Divines, who have been heated and heightened with the greatest zeal of Opposition to the Pope, as the Antichrist, yet have believed a Pope to have ascended from the Papal Chair to a Throne in Heaven. Had my Education, my Acquaintance, the several Circumstances and Concurrences been the same to me as to this person from whom I now most of all dissent, that which is now his sense and state, might have been mine. Have the same just, equal, tender respects and thoughts, with the same allowance, of one another, which thou requirest from him to thyself."

3. Calvinists and Arminians were at daggers drawn in terry's day. He was true to his own counsel in honouring the "Persons engaged on both sides," and in appreciating the special aspect of the truth for which each was contending. "It is the design of one part to heighten the Grace of God by its freedom and peculiarity; of the

other, to enlarge the glory of this Grace by its extent and amplitude." "One admires or adores absoluteness, the sovreignty of God; the other, the goodness." Then the one grows jealous lest something should be ascribed to man which detracts from the power of God; and the other lest something should be ascribed to God which stains His moral glory. But "the day will come when men shall say, Blessed is he who comes in the name of the Lord—Blessed is the peacemaker who shall reconcile, on the one hand, the freedom and peculiarity of the Grace of God unto a full amplitude and extent, so raising its sweetness to a perfect height; and, on the other, shall (so) bring into mutual embraces the sovreignty or absoluteness of God and His goodness (as) that the sovreignty and absoluteness may be sovreign and absolutely good; (as) that the goodness alone may be absolute and sovereign."

4. It is evident that Sterry himself hoped to be this reconciler, or at least his forerunner. Love is first, and must be given the first place, if Christians are to attain a true knowledge of God and a true fellowship in God with one another. This is His message, and He is full of longing that it may be received. "Let love instruct and prompt thee, gentle Reader, to think that the worthless author . . . may have been led by a sacred beam of this love touching his heart from on high, so near unto the borders of the happy regions and kingdoms of Divine Truth as to discover *all to be heaven there.* . . . Then let the sweet waters of this Divine Love, from its own fountain sprinkled upon thine heart, raise this candid belief in thee, that as a pair of silver-feathered Doves flying before Æneas, guided him to the tree laden with golden boughs, in the midst of a thick and obscure

wood,[1] so this *Discourse*, aiming at a resemblance of those beautiful and lovely birds, sacred to love, in a whiteness of unspotted candour, may be a birth of Love, though weak, and flying low, sent forth to allure and guide thee into the everlasting Heavens of divine truth and goodness." But "perhaps some one will say, who is this that thus preacheth Love to the world? Is he a Dove washt in milk?" Far from it in his own eyes. "No, the only character here is that of *a voice in the wilderness*— a wilderness of many Deformities and Distractions, within as well as without—crying, Prepare ye the way of Divine Love, make straight paths for it, by bringing down every mountain of Vanity and Pride, by filling up the Vallies of low, dejected, lost, despairing Spirits. He who thus cries to you, too frequently, too deeply, hath pierced the side of this Love; yet still from the wounded heart—through the wounds—water and blood flow to wash off the stains of this blood upon him; and by this blood as a Balsam, as a cordial, as a Spring of Life, all at once to heal his wounds, to infuse new vigour and joy into his spirits, to renew life in his heart, even out of Death itself into immortality. This is the Innocency and Wisdom which make them blessed who aspire to it; who, as often as they fail in their duty of loving every other person as themselves, are sensible of the guilt of breaking the whole law—which is summed up in these two great commandments—and maketh them (as) inseparable as the substance and the shadow in the sunshine, or as the Fountain and the Stream, or the Sun and the similitude of the Sun in the light surrounding it: to love God with (all) ourselves and to love our neighbour (as) ourselves."

[1] Sterry seems to be aware of his own obscurity or rather of that of his subject.

IV

Sterry wished he "had a hundred mouths, a hundred tongues, a voice like thunder; like the voice of God which rends the rocks," if thereby he might be able to move to repentance the warring heart of the "Christian World" of his day; and "so quench that fire which" (said he) "turns upon your estates, your houses, your relations, your bodies, your souls, even to the nethermost Hell." But he was a solitary unheeded voice. Most of the few who paused to listen passed on to scoff. Only one here and there felt constrained to stay. One of these was Jeremiah White (1629–1707) who, in publishing a volume of his master's sermons, wrote a preface which he afterwards enlarged into a separate treatise under the title a *Persuasive to Moderation*—a plea for Christian tolerance of remarkable eloquence and force, and bearing witness on every page to the source of its inspiration. Another disciple might be claimed, perhaps, in Sir Harry Vane, Jr., whose work *The Retired Man's Meditations* (1655) was a sympathetic enforcement of the same plea which, for its breadth, provoked dissent from Richard Baxter [1] and prompted his fulsome admirer, Henry Stubbs (1632–1676) (who also professed to be for a "Toleration of all Opinions," and wrote his *Essay in Defence of the Good Old Cause* partly for that purpose), to assail Baxter in a scurrilous pamphlet (called *Malice Rebuked*) from which all Christian tolerance was absent. A third disciple [2] who published a second volume of Sterry's sermons, indulged a faint hope that enough copies might be sold to warrant the issue of a

---

[1] *Key for Catholicks* (1659).
[2] Perhaps R. Rooch, who edited White's *Persuasive*.

further volume; but as this never came out we may infer that the former found few purchasers. As Jeremiah White said—"it has still been the lot of the divinest births and appearances of God in this lower world to be more solitary and neglected as to an outward pomp and attendance. They are reserved for the glory and triumph of another day." So far Sterry's day seems not to have come. Yet the leaven of his spirit cannot have perished. It must have worked together with other elements of man's nobler mind; and must have had its effect in bringing men to a keener sense of what is laid upon their conscience by the Christian law of love. Possibly to Sterry's humble soul this would have seemed a not insufficient reward of all his travail. But one cannot but wish him better known—especially by those who have not resigned the belief that the thoughts of a mystic may be vehicles of light from the inmost shrine of truth.[1]

[1] Except one or two sermons, nothing of Sterry's was published during his life; but in—

(1) 1675 there appeared *A Discourse of the Freedom of the Will* (printed under difficulties, partly from fear that it might "be stifled in the birth"). Fol. pp. 30 (Preface), 245.

(2) 1683—*The Rise, Race and Royalty of the Kingdom of God in the Soul of Man*... (sermons). 8vo. pp. 575, Address to Reader 23 pp. by Jonathan White.

(3) 1710. The appearance of God in the Gospel and other sermons, with an explanation of the Trinity, a short catechism, and five letters concerning the Trinity, Christ's sufferings, satisfaction and Resurrection (these letters give the pith of his teaching). 8vo. pp. 480.

A second part of this vol., on Virtue, Eternity, etc., was promised, if called for; but there was no demand.

A number of his "Prayers" is included in a collection which appeared in 1785, 8vo.

EPILOGUE

I

TULLOCH's "general estimate" of the Cambridge men in the last chapter of his book [1] is fairly comprehensive; and just, on the whole. But, under the head of "Defects," he has some remarks which cannot be taken without question. Thus, it is true that, in their quotations from the Platonists, they failed to appreciate the differences between Plato and Plotinus, or between Plotinus and Proclus. They passed from one to the other indiscriminately, and showed little or no critical insight, no perception of the penetrating changes which had gradually transformed the mental world of 250 B.C. into the mental world of A.D. 450.

This is true, but they did not lose much by the mistake if—as I have pointed out above (p. 23)—they used the Platonic writers not to establish their doctrines so much as to illustrate them, just as a modern writer or speaker might quote out of his favourite authors, from Chaucer to Tennyson, to light up, or press home, views arrived at independently. The Platonic writers were a new literature to the Cambridge men. It was delightful to read them and to find so much in which they seemed to anticipate their own best thought, and so to confirm their beliefs

[1] *Rational Theology . . . in the Seventeenth Century*, vol. ii. chap. vi.

in man's natural capacity for knowing God and His truth. But when Tulloch says that "their minds were drenched with the speculations of the Alexandrian School in all its forms," and that "the theosophic reveries of this school" "fitted more aptly their supersensual imaginations" than "the vivacity, inquisitiveness, common-sense, and dialectical badinage of the Platonic Socrates," [1] one must demur. Not to ask what is meant here by the Alexandrian school,[2] he is confounding Whichcote, Smith and Cudworth with More; and is unfair even to More. For not even More was ever drenched with Alexandrian speculations. His speculations were stimulated much more by the Prophecies and the Cabbala. It is a question whether he knew very much of Plotinus or Proclus, at any time. Certainly his later extravagances owed little or nothing to either of them; while as to the others, Cudworth is the only one who borrowed from Platonism in any wholesale fashion. He did so in his effort to elaborate an explanation of the Trinity, and in his theory of a mundane soul (*intellectus Agens*). Smith, too, argued for the latter (in a casual way). But these things hardly touched the core of their thought. They were its mere trimmings. What they held to be vital for faith and life, came to them from a higher Teacher—though it was good to catch the echo of his voice in the Platonists. And if this can be said of Cudworth and Smith it is still more obviously true of Whichcote, in whose sermons and aphorisms there is not even a faint "Platonic tincture." Nothing could be

---

[1] Ibid., pp. 479, 480.
[2] Which, as a phrase, might refer to the Christian School of Clemens or the heathen school of Hypatia.

farther from the mark than to speak of him as "drenched with the speculations of the Alexandrian School in all its forms." This is not the only point in which Tulloch needs some qualifying. Thus, he goes too far when he says, "ALL their writings not only smell of the academic lamp, but have the operosity and cumbrousness of the school rather than the finish of the thinker who has been trained, but has forgot his training in the consciousness of accomplishment and power which it has left behind. They carry their academical trappings with them whatever they do. They crowd their books with specimens of all the intellectual furniture which they gathered in the course of their studies." [1]

There is exaggeration here even with respect to More of whom it is truest. It is less true of Cudworth—though he had naturally a heavy style. John Smith sprinkled his eloquent periods with Greek, Latin, and even Hebrew sentences; but by no means to the detriment of his style, to those who could understand, as his hearers and intended readers mostly could. It was a fault much in fashion; and, in his case, was a fault redeemed by the admirable fitness of his quotations. To Whichcote it scarcely applies at all. There is no smell of the lamp anywhere in his sermons—with the rare exception of two or three which, from internal evidence, can safely be referred to some academic occasion. Allowing for the patent fact that many passages have been badly reported, the sermons bespeak a mind which was like an overflowing spring for spontaneity and simplicity and clearness. No hearer could miss his meaning any more than a modern reader can do. The twelve

[1] Ibid., pp. 476, 477.

"centuries" of Aphorisms collected from them, and his table-talk, serve for sufficient proof.

But Tulloch's most serious mistake, I think, is in *taxing all* the Cambridge men with the "credulity" of More and Glanvil (1636–1680) concerning "Ghosts and apparitions," or at least concerning their use to demonstrate "the Supernatural." This was a grave fault in More; but the others had little, or no, share in it. Their sober rationalism held them clear of it and made them sceptical—in an age when some of the keenest intellects, Sir Matthew Hale, for example, did not escape the snare. Nor is it correct to say that their rationalism, while not equal to the defeat of superstition on the one hand, attempted an impossible task, on the other.

"They essayed to verify the Divine, not merely to witness it to man's reason and conscience, but to construe it into a Philosophy and rear a Science of Religion." [1]

This was surely a purpose which never entered even into their dreams. They did maintain, on the ground of insight and experience, that man is inveterately religious; that the great elementary facts of religion—God, Duty, and Immortality—are disclosed to every reverent, humble and obedient soul; that such discoveries of the natural reason are cleared and confirmed by the light of Christ; and that it is man's true wisdom (or philosophy) to order his life accordingly. But they had no thought of constructing a Philosophy, and rearing a science of religion. From first to last, their interest lay within the sphere of religion as a light, and motive, for life. They were philosophers simply in the sense of believing, with

[1] Ibid., p. 485.

all their heart, that it was easier to give a natural account of religion, rightly understood, than of anything else.

II

What has been the influence of the Cambridge School?

It is not a question easy to answer.

When one thinks of the men who, generation after generation, passed through the hands of Whichcote, Smith, Cudworth and More—all noted as excellent and popular tutors—one cannot but imagine that many of these fresh minds must have been moulded by the spirit and ideals of the new movement—and, afterwards, have done something to propagate it in the social, political, or clerical circles to which they removed. But definite examples are rare. One such was that of Edward Fowler, a Presbyterian chaplain, who became Rector of Northill in Bedfordshire, and ultimately Bishop of Gloucester. He was scoffed at by John Bunyan and his fellows because he did not come out in 1662; and he defended himself [1] by reasons drawn from the theory and practice of his Cambridge teachers, which said in effect, 'the State has a right to use its discretion in the matter of allowing or forbidding the observance of things confessedly indifferent; and the loyal churchman should obey. Better yield too much than turn your back on the Church, and encourage a schismatic temper.' Such was the Cambridge position; and the Nonconformist had a good answer to it. But that it might be held conscien-

---

[1] In a volume entitled *The Design of Christianity* . . . (1671).

tiously was what the Nonconformist did not always recognise. It would have lessened bitterness, and made accommodation more possible, had he done so.

The direct influence of individual members of the School is easier to trace than its collective influence. Thus, Whichcote's influence on John Smith, and Smith's on Simon Patrick (1626–1707) and John Worthington (1618–1671); More's on Joseph Glanvil (1636–1680) and Peter Sterry and John Norris (1657–1711); Cudworth's on John Locke (1632–1704); Whichcote's, again, on John Wilkins (1614–1672), and John Tillotson (1630–1694), and (through Tillotson) on Burnet (1643–1715), and (by means of his published Sermons) on the third Lord Shaftesbury (1671–1713), author of the *Characteristics*: all this, and more of the kind,[1] is traceable. In this way, no doubt, the collective influence of the School was transmitted and circulated. But, inasmuch as it necessarily mingled with other streams of tendency which might be flowing in the same direction, we cannot mark off its course and range with precision. Bearing this in mind, we may say, nevertheless, that some of the most salient developments of the eighteenth century—Rationalism, Deism, Scripturalism, Moralism, Tolerance—went the way and took the form they did, because directed, more or less, by the principles or spirit of the Cambridge men. There is no space here for elaborate proof. We can do little more than point it out as a fact.

[1] It seems to me certain, from internal evidence, that Henry Scougal (1650–1678), the brilliant and saintly young Scotsman, Professor of Divinity at King's College, Aberdeen, and author of *The Life of God in the Soul of Man*, had read, and been influenced by, John Smith, the first edition of whose *Discourses* appeared in 1660. See, e.g., the extracts from his book quoted by Professor Micklem in *God's Freeman* (1922), pp. 109, 111, 115.

1. It is strange to find Mark Pattison (in his "Tendencies of Religious Thought in England")[1] proposing to take Locke's *Reasonableness of Christianity* (1695) as "the commencement of rationalism in England." He adds a saving clause, that, of course, "there were Rationalists before Locke," e.g. "Hales of Eton and other Arminians"; and perhaps the latter phrase was meant to cover the Cambridge men. But these apparently were not worth specifying as pioneers of the tendency which attained its first culmination in Locke. There should be no need to say, in the light of our study, that the usual accuracy of Pattison has, for once, failed him. Indeed, one is almost inclined to wonder if he had so much as heard of the Cambridge men, when he could quote the following passage from Locke's *Essay* and not detect the voice—nay, in part, even the words of Whichcote and Smith and Culverwel: "Reason is natural revelation, whereby the Father of Light and fountain of all knowledge, communicates to mankind that portion of truth which he has laid within the reach of their natural faculties. Revelation is natural reason enlarged by a new set of discoveries communicated by God immediately, which Reason vouches the truth of, by the testimony and proofs it gives that they come from God. So that he that takes away Reason to make a way for Revelation, puts out the light of both, and does much the same as if he would persuade a man to put out his eyes, the better to receive the remote light of an invisible star by a telescope."

There cannot be much doubt that, during his Oxford student life (1652–1660), Locke imbibed, "to some

[1] In *Essays and Reviews*.

o

extent, at any rate, the opinions of the Cambridge Latitudinarians." [1]

It is certain that, later, he made the personal acquaintance of Cudworth in London, and either from Cudworth himself, or more fully, from Damaris his daughter, learnt all about the new movement. And it is difficult to suppose that he could be a close friend of Tillotson, as he was, and not go to hear Whichcote, the preacher of St. Lawrence Jewry whom Tillotson so admired and to whom he was an assistant. In fact we are expressly told that Whichcote was Locke's favourite preacher, nor is it at all unlikely that he often met him in private life, during the years, from 1667 to 1675, when Locke had his home mostly in London. Thus, his connection by several links with the Cambridge men is beyond question; and their influence upon him—an influence which, so far as his Rationalism is concerned, he never outgrew—is demonstrable. [2]

We are asked to believe by Fox Bourne that Damaris Cudworth was led by Locke "to diverge widely from her father" [3]; but on the point of their common rationalism she is emphatic enough:

"He (Locke) was always in the greatest and the smallest affairs of human life, as well as in speculative opinions, disposed to follow Reason, whosoever it were

---

[1] Fox Bourne's *Life of Locke*, vol. i., p. 77.

[2] See Von Hertling, *John Locke und die Schule von Cambridge* (1892), third chapter.

[3] Locke taught her to find the true genius of Christianity not in Neo-Platonism (like her father) but in Utilitarianism. (*Life*, i. 477.) The remark is singularly inept: for Cudworth's test of Christianity was just its power of moral salvation, in which Neo-Platonism was lacking. Nor did Locke mean more than this by Utilitarianism.

that suggested it, he being ever a faithful servant—I
had almost said a slave—to Truth, never abandoning
her for anything else, and following her, for her own
sake, purely."[1]

His view of Reason, too, in relation to Revelation, was
entirely that of Whichcote and his friends—"Whatsoever
is Divine Revelation ought to overrule our opinions, prejudices and interests. Whatsoever God hath revealed is
certainly true. No doubt can be made of it. But whether
it be a Divine Revelation or no, Reason must judge,
which can never permit the mind to reject a greater
evidence for that which is less evident, or prefer less
certainty to greater. There can be no evidence that any
Traditional Revelation is of Divine Original in the word
we receive it in, and in the sense we understand it, so
clear and so certain as those of the Principles of
religion."[2] "No Proposition can be received for Divine
Revelation, or obtain the assent due to all such, if it
be contradictory to our clear intuitive knowledge."[3]
Compare the statement of Tillotson[4]:

"All our reasonings about Revelation are necessarily
gathered by our natural notions about religion, and,
therefore, he who sincerely desires to do the will of God
is not apt to be imposed on by vain pretences of divine
revelation; but if any doctrine be proposed to him which
pretended to come from God, he measures it by those
sure and steady notions which he has of Divine Nature
and perfections. He will consider the nature and tendency

---

[1] Von Hertling, *John Locke und die Schule von Cambridge*
(1892), third chapter, p. 540.
[2] *Essay on the Human Understanding*, Bk. 4, chap. 18, § 10.
[3] Ibid., § 5.
[4] Quoted by Pattison.

of it, or whether it be a doctrine according to godliness such as is agreeable to the Divine nature and perfections, and tends to make us like unto God; if it be not, though an angel should bring it from Heaven, he would not receive it." There is evident agreement here between Tillotson and Locke; and the former did but echo what Whichcote always said on the same point. Locke, it is safe to say, focussed the ruling ideas of his age as no other man did—focussed and radiated the heat and light of them, enriched, or at least coloured, by the vigorous originality of his own mind. He became, in an exceptional manner, the intellectual guide of the eighteenth century, and its most potent influence. His philosophical standpoint, with its momentous implications, was his own—was his special contribution to the world of thought; and was that in which the Cambridge men had least affinity with him; but, all the same, he was the chief channel through whom their spirit passed onward, and imprinted itself, with formative force, on the "Seculum Rationalisticum."

2. We have seen the place assigned to the Christian Revelation by the Cambridge men, as that which confirmed and completed the light of nature. Locke also assigned to it the same high place:—"I gratefully receive and rejoice in the light of Revelation which sets me at rest in many things, the manner whereof my poor Reason can by no means make out to me. I readily believe whatever God has declared, tho' my Reason find difficulties in it which I cannot master." (Third letter to Stillingfleet.)

He is thankful for it especially, as they were, because it has strengthened the assurance of forgiveness, and clarified the will of God, and changed the "obscure glimmering, the uncertain hopes," of a future life, furnished by the light of nature, into "clearness and certainty" through the resurrection of Jesus Christ. Thus, the Cambridge men again offered a lead which was widely followed. For it became the habit of Christian preachers and writers generally, if they were of the progressive sort, to set forth Christianity as an appendix, and a key, to natural religion.

"This was the point which the Christian Defenders laboured most, to construct the bridge which should unite the revealed to the natural. They never demur to making the natural the basis on which Christianity rests; to considering the natural knowledge of God as the starting-point both of the individual mind and of the human race. This assumption is necessary to their scheme, in which revelation is an argument addressed to the reason. Christianity is a résumé of the knowledge of God already attained by reason and a disclosure of further truths. These further truths could not have been thought out by reason, but when divinely communicated they approve themselves to the same reason which has already put us in possession of so much."[1] Pattison quotes Butler (1692–1752), Warburton (1698–1779), Ferguson and others as all arguing in this way, that is, *in the way of Whichcote* who, when speaking of the Deists as mere naturalists, declared:

"They are Catholicks; they entertain all that ever was in the world from God; they only stick at the Revelation and the Superstructure. To these I would say, 'You do well so far as you go; you do well to entertain all that

[1] Pattison.

God hath laid the foundation for; you do well to follow
the light of Reason, but do you think that God can do no
more? Do you think that God did all at once?' I do not
blame these men that they are very slow of faith, that
they will not believe further than they see reason: for
nothing is more impotent than to be light of faith. . . .
But we must be ready to hear when God shall speak."
He adds, that the Doctrines of the "meer naturalists"
are "equivalent to the seven precepts of Noah. Yet there
is no reason why the grace of God bringing salvation,
should not be superadded, that teacheth men to live
soberly, righteously and godly. . . . This establisheth
the other."

But there was a flaw in the argument which gravely
weakened its effect, viz. it harped so much on what a
man may learn by natural light about God and His will;
and on the sufficiency of this for guidance and even
salvation, that he might well be tempted to ask, "Why
should more be given or required? You admit that by
natural light we may know there is a God, and that He
is infinitely good, and that His forgiveness waits on
repentance, and that He freely imparts the grace of
His spirit to the penitent, is not that enough? What
need of a superadditional revelation?"

And when it was replied: "Certainly one might have
supposed it to be enough; but, as a matter of fact, such
a revelation has been given, has been given in the
Scriptures which are the Word of God, and, therefore,
must be received," was not the inquirer entitled to ask
further, "How do you know that the Scriptures are the
Word of God?"; and, when the answer came, "They are
proved to be such by prophecies fulfilled and miracles

performed as well as by intrinsic marks of truth," immediately the whole wide field of controversy about evidences was opened—controversy in which the combatants lost themselves in noise and smoke. Nor could the battle be decided until it came to be seen and acknowledged: (*a*) that too much had been handed over to natural light in the first instance, or, in other words, that there had been ascribed to it not a little which was derived from Scripture; (*b*) that the chief end of Scripture was to record a revelation growing more and more to its perfect day in Christ; and (*c*) that the acceptance of this depends not on miracles and prophecies but on that witness of the spirit which is given in the experience of a humble and obedient heart. But *that* lay beyond the orbit of eighteenth century thought; and here we simply note how the teaching of Whichcote and his fellows, transmitted through the contracting medium of Locke's colder intellect, supplied occasion and warrant to the Deists.

We may note three other points as suggestive of the Cambridge influence.

3. By the middle of the eighteenth century "Dogmatic Theology," says Pattison, "had ceased to exist." Apologetics had taken its place. But another interest, also, had taken its place. The reaction against Dogmatic Theology was occasioned partly by a growing desire to base religious belief on Scripture alone; and to keep strictly to its literal teaching. If Scripture was the Protestant *regula fidei*, this was evidently a sound principle; and the tendency of Churchmen to make Creed, etc., obligatory might render it a dead letter. So Chillingworth said (1637) in the famous words:

"The presumptuous imposing of the senses of men

upon the words of God, the special senses of men upon the general words of God, and laying them upon men's consciences under the equal penalty of death and damnation, the vain conceit that we can speak of the things of God better than in the words of God . . . hath been the only fountain of all the schisms of the Church. . . ." Whichcote said just the same in his answer to Tuckney, and in many passages of his sermons. For him and all the Cambridge men the authority of Scripture as the Word of God was unquestioned; the authority of Creeds and Fathers was altogether secondary. The plain straightforward sense of the Scripture text—construed by reason with reverent "application" to the spirit of God, the author of Scripture—must determine faith. The imposition of anything else as "orthodox" was a source of fatal mischief. "Determinations beyond Scripture have indeed enlarged faith, but lessened Charity and multiplied Divisions." (Aphorism 981.) "Nothing is of faith that is not in Scripture, nothing is necessary as otherwise expressed; nothing is certain, as further made out. We may live in Christian Love and Union without consent and agreement in non-scriptural expressions or forms of words." (Aphorism 1161.) Whether Locke repeated this with conscious assent to Whichcote or not, he did in effect repeat it:

"It would be strange indeed, if God who made the tongue and organs of speech, who gave us all the use of language, cannot be understood when He declares His will to man without the help of an interpreter who thus must know the thought of God better than God Himself. As if the words of God, being obscure, man could light us there; as if the mind of creatures could be more

erudite than the mind that formed them! [1] This exclusive
dependence on the letter of Scripture had great results.
For one thing, it initiated the Arian Movement. Of that
movement Dr. Samuel Clarke (1675–1729), Rector of
St. James's, Westminster, may fairly be described as
the pioneer—though Thomas Emlyn (1663–1741) was
somewhat earlier in the field [2]; and his *Scripture
Doctrine of the Trinity* exhibits in its title the ground
on which he based himself. Discarding all previous
historical formulations of the Trinity, he professed to
bring his mind as a *tabula rasa* to the New Testament,
understood in its plain and proper sense. The Semi-arian
conclusion at which he arrived was (he said) something
forced upon him by the evidence. Locke and Sir Isaac
Newton (1642–1727) wound up their no less "impartial"
study of Scripture at much the same goal. Their view
of the Trinity, however, was not known till later. It was
Clarke who discredited the acceptance of "mere Scripture" as a sufficient "rule of faith"; and started the
fight of subscribers against non-subscribers, which came
to a head at the Salters' Hall Conference in 1719. The
hinge of that conference was the question *not* do you or
do you not believe in the Trinity? but will you subscribe
the orthodox statements of it? Many of those who refused to subscribe claimed to be good Trinitarians. All
they contended for was the right to frame their belief
according to the New Testament and express it in strictly
Scripture terms. Their position appeared to be inexpugn-
able, inasmuch as both sides rendered equal verbal
homage to Scripture. But the subscribers were moved

[1] *Infalliblis Scripturæ Interpres non Necessarius* (1661).
[2] *Vindication of the Worship of the Lord Jesus Christ on
Unitarian Principles* (1706).

by a sure instinct. As matter of history, the devotees of the Scripture rule of faith drifted more and more into Arianism, and did so for the simple reason that their method of studying the New Testament led up to it. For what they did was to collect all references to the person of Christ, and attach to each the same degree of importance—or rather attach a preponderating importance to certain passages (like 1 Cor. xv. 28, and Philip. ii. 9–11) without any perception of the fact that the material for a true Christology lies not so much in specific words of the New Testament as in the developing Christian consciousness of Christ's unique relation to God and man which is there gradually unveiled.

The Cambridge men would have found themselves driven to a similar conclusion with regard to Christ and the Trinity if they had tried to work out their reading of the New Testament into a system. But, happily, circumstances did not put this demand upon them as they did upon the Arians; and, besides, their mind was much more under the control of orthodox prepossessions. Nevertheless, it was Locke and the Arians who followed up the logic of their rigid Scripturalism.

4. Pattison observes, as to the moral character of the eighteenth century, that "after making every allowance for the exaggeration of religious rhetoric, etc., there seems to remain some real evidence for ascribing to that age a more than usual moral licence and contempt of external restraint. It is the concurrent testimony of men of all parties"; and he quotes six flagrant signs of this set forth by a contemporary layman, David Hartley.[1] Of

[1] See first chapter of Lecky's *History of England in the Eighteenth Century*.

course there were thousands of exceptions to the prevailing looseness—thousands of men and women who
lived quiet, orderly and sober lives. But they were, for
the most part, hidden away in the shade of country
homes. To the casual eye iniquity had burst all bounds.
And the Churches exerted little or no counteractive
force. Their ministers were, in the majority of cases,
so many moral cyphers—if not worse.[1] Their salt had
lost its savour, their light was hidden under the bushel
of a pharisaic orthodoxy. Never more fierce for the so-
called saving doctrines of the Gospel, they were never
more antinomian in conduct. But the spirit of the Cambridge men, so utterly hostile to any view of religion
which disparaged the moral imperatives of the Gospel,
was not dead. It spoke through Locke who in this respect,
above all, was their disciple; it spoke through not a few,
within the establishment, who drew it from its earlier
representatives, such as Tillotson and Wilkins; it spoke
emphatically through those same Arians whom it
soon became the fashion to blaspheme as "a pest," "a
gangrene," "a plague," "a fungus." No one can doubt
this who has taken pains to get at the facts. Like the
Cambridge men they found their moral earnestness
enlightened and intensified by an honest study of the
Scriptures, especially the New Testament; like the Cambridge men they were led to lay an ever-deepening stress
on the moral side of true religion, by disgust at the
ethical barrenness of theological dogmatism; like the
Cambridge men, again, they were "gibbeted" as traitors
to the gospel. How many of them had any acquaintance
with the sermons of Whichcote or Smith we cannot say:

[1] See Cowper's *Task*, Book II.

probably very few. But they read Locke. They were largely his disciples in Philosophy, and his *Reasonableness of Christianity* was one of their classics. By his means then, if not directly, the moral dynamic of the Cambridge School continued to act in the degenerate life of England. It was a service for which the Arian preachers and teachers deserved a credit which they have not received—though its effects were never widely visible.

5. Lastly, in no way did the influence of the Cambridge men avail more powerfully than in promoting the temper and practice of toleration. True, the ecclesiastical policy of 1662 took no account of them, and even the policy of 1689 was not in line with what they dreamed of— viz. a Church so broad in its definition of fundamentals, and so generous in its ceremonial requirements, as to make it an inviting home to all reasonable persons. True, also, that the temper of the Church after 1662 had never been so exacting, so stupid, so embittered against Dissenters. But Tillotson, Wilkins, Simon Patrick, Fowler, Pearson, who owned them, more or less, as their leaders, and—with perhaps undue regard to the dictates of prudence—acted for justice and peace, had many followers, at least among the town clergy and the cultivated laity. So many opposing forces were at work that, looked at from the outside, the result seemed chaos; but Siloam's gentle stream, with its promise of gladness for the city of God, was flowing and gathering strength underneath. The Toleration Act and its later extensions were not, so to speak, eruptive events. Their coming had been prepared for by an indefinite number of men like those just mentioned. And here once

more the chief agent was Locke. "When he was barely
twenty-eight years old and still only an Oxford student,
his great desire, as regards ecclesiastical matters, was
for a national church so simple in its creeds and articles
that it could include or comprehend nearly all who had
any religious opinions at all, while he also desired the
completest toleration of every honest person who should
find the broadest of all possible broad churches too
narrow for him." [1]

This was his idea of religious freedom on the political
side, and it corresponds precisely to that of Whichcote.
But the personal side, or the generous temper of Whichcote expressed in scores of his Aphorisms—e.g. "Universal charity is a thing final in religion"—is no less
present in Locke. While, in the presumed interest of
civic safety, he could not see his way to enfranchise a
Papist or an Atheist, he thought of them with kindness;
his personal relations with them were friendly; and he
would have been the last to doubt the possibility of
their salvation. He was (like the Cambridge men) entirely free from the *odium theologicum* so rampant
around him. And this of itself seems to cast doubt on
the statement of his biographer that his exemplar in
the matter of tolerance was Dr. John Owen (1616–1683),
under whom, when Head of Christ Church, he lived
some years at Oxford. If, indeed, the statement had
reference to political toleration only, something might
be said for it. For as to this Owen was sound enough.
"Gospel constitutions"—he said—"in the case of heresy
or error seem not to favour any course of violence, I
mean of civil penalties. . . . Admonitions or, in the last

[1] Fox Bourne, vol. i., p. 173.

resort, excommunications are the fitting punishment and that by the Church, not imprisoning, banishing, slaying either by Church or State." [1]

These are the words of a good Independent; and if he spoke in a similar strain at Oxford, Locke was certain to agree. But Locke does not say that he ever heard him speak thus, nor does he acknowledge any indebtedness to Owen for his own breadth of view. On the other hand, if he became aware of Owen's attitude on that Committee of Divines which was nominated by the House of Commons in November 1654, to determine the limits of permissible toleration under the "Instrument of Government"—an attitude strangely misapprehended by Fox Bourne—Locke cannot possibly have sympathised with it. Owen took the phrase in question—"Such as profess faith in God by Jesus Christ"—and so hampered its simplicity by some twenty qualifications, that there could have been no breadth at all in the church-state if they had taken effect. Owen, in fact, detested heresy and threw a wide net for heretics. Locke, however, drew them all within his charity if they were sincere; and herein he declared the real source of his inspiration. In the Cambridge men he found the idea of a broadly comprehensive Church; and, still better, the warm glow of a richly comprehensive love. The former gave place to his own great scheme of Toleration, when comprehension was refused; the latter he cherished and practised to his life's end. In and through him, therefore, the Cambridge mustard seed grew at length into a great tree.

Yet under one aspect the Cambridge men had no

---

[1] Appendix to his sermon on the execution of Charles I., quoted by Fox Bourne, i. p. 70.

apparent survival. As they conceived it, Reason was a divine light, or the organ of a Divine spirit; but in the prevailing thought of the eighteenth century, it became another name for common sense. As they conceived it, morality was the fruit of a divine life—a life hid with Christ in God, and the vision of God was the sure reward of a pure heart; but in the prevailing thought of the eighteenth century, morality tended more and more to become another name for utility, and the vision of God the unpractical dream of a mystic. Thus, the highest part of them may be said to have vanished; and Locke, with a religious experience subservient to his clear-cut understanding, helped to speed its flight.

Its recovery, in a modified and fuller form, has been the attainment of a later day.

FINIS

INDEX

P
215